Counselling Techniques
for Managers

Counselling Techniques for Managers

Hilary Walmsley

KOGAN
PAGE

Thank you to my family, Greg Paytosh and Rebecca Kurth for kind support and valuable comments.

First published in 1994

Apart from any fair dealing for the purposes of research or private study, or criticism or review, as permitted under the Copyright, Designs and Patents Act, 1988, this publication may only be reproduced, stored or transmitted, in any form or by any means, with the prior permission in writing of the publishers, or in the case of reprographic reproduction in accordance with the terms of licences issued by the Copyright Licensing Agency. Enquiries concerning reproduction outside those terms should be sent to the publishers at the undermentioned address:

Kogan Page Limited
120 Pentonville Road
London N1 9JN

© Hilary Walmsley, 1994

British Library Cataloguing in Publication Data

A CIP record for this book is available from the British Library.

ISBN 0 7494 1281 X

Typeset by DP Photosetting, Aylesbury, Bucks.
Printed and bound in England by Clays Ltd, St Ives plc.

Contents

About the Author

Hilary Walmsley BSc, MSc, MBA is a consultant in business psychology, specialising in management development, based in London. She consults, coaches and runs public and private tutorials in counselling skills and other personal and management development skills.

About the book

As a manager, what is your style of dealing with subordinates? Before reading on, stop and think about what you would actually say to your subordinates in the following situations:

- A staff member approaches you because she is having difficulty getting along with a colleague on a project team.
- You need to meet with one of your staff who has not followed the correct procedure for organising his holiday periods.
- A designer on your team is losing her creative streak.
- You are receiving complaints from job candidates regarding the interviewing methods of one of your most successful supervisors.
- A subordinate tells you he is having relationship problems at home with his partner and doesn't know what to do.

Do you always manage situations and solve problems using the same style? Do you stop and think about the approach you are using or do you habitually attack most problems in the same manner? Are you aware of the different styles of management available for you to use – for example, various ways of problem solving, and methods of developing and motivating employees?

Management development today needs to focus on training managers in the *conscious* use of different styles. That is, managers must be trained to stop and think about which style they are going to apply to a given situation, and to be cognisant of *why* they have chosen that style. The approach chosen should correspond to the needs of the situation.

Using counselling skills is the most effective way to implement the modern participative style of management – empowering your subordinates in order to get the best results. The techniques of counselling are becoming increasingly essential for achieving peak performance in today's changing work environment. They are also very useful for improving interpersonal skills generally, so you can use these techniques to improve your relationships outside work as well.

Unfortunately, the concept of counselling is generally very misunderstood. Some managers mistakenly assume that they are already using counselling skills; others simply do not understand how counselling works and what its benefits are in the work environment. This is hardly surprising, given that many people in business have not been exposed to a counselling style of operating. The counselling techniques used by professional psychologists can be used in an amateur way by managers to great effect, but only if the manager understands the concept of counselling, recognises the implications of the skills he or she is applying, and knows when it is appropriate to use these skills.

The word 'counselling' can frighten traditional business people. It doesn't sound very business oriented. But the forward-thinking companies and managers who are coming to understand the concept and beginning to utilise the skills of counselling are the ones who will harness the resources within their employees – the key to success in the future. Managerial application of *real* counselling skills at work is still a relatively new concept for business, and one that has tremendous potential for increasing individuals' and therefore companies' effectiveness.

This book is intended to help you as a manager or supervisor to develop yourself and increase your performance management effectiveness by being able to apply counselling skills in appropriate situations. The specific objectives of the book are as follows:

- To convince you of the benefits and value of using counselling skills at work.
- To give you an overall understanding of:
  — the process of counselling;
  — the results of counselling;
  — how counselling differs from other types of helping;
  — how 'applying counselling skills' differs from 'pure counselling'.
- To provide you with practical instruction on:
  — recognising a situation which calls for the application of counselling techniques;
  — learning to use the specific skills;
  — implementing counselling skills in your own workplace in a variety of specific work situations.

Many business books have been written on management development, change management, and improving communication and interpersonal skills. There are, however, very few books on one of the most potent tactics for achieving all these goals – managers acquiring counselling skills and applying them in the workplace. Books on counselling are found in the psychology areas of libraries and bookshops, rarely in the business sections. The author hopes that this book will help to bridge the gap.

Disclaimer

Throughout the book the words 'manager' and 'subordinate' have been used. Unfortunately there is no word in the English vocabulary to describe those who work for a manager which does not sound awkward. Employee, junior and underling sound even less appropriate. The counselling relationship is characterised by equality, which the words 'manager' and 'subordinate' do not connote, but they are accurate words to describe the participants – more so than 'counsellor' and 'client', which sound clinical.

Names of individuals and organisations in case examples have been changed in order to protect privacy.

PART ONE

Why use counselling skills?

1

Applying Counselling Skills in the Workplace

There now exists a growing managerial awareness of the increasing importance of giving 'people issues' attention and consideration equal to that given to financial, logistical and customer issues. The methods, or 'how to', of addressing people issues are not yet well established, however. Using counselling techniques is the most effective method, and is becoming essential for managers who want to achieve peak performance. Counselling skills are only now beginning to receive the attention warranted from mainstream managers and supervisors, an interest heightened by the current focus on performance and productivity.

Over the past two decades, droves of managers have attended training programmes aimed to improve their management style and their skills in handling people. Interpersonal, communication, assertiveness, facilitation and presentation skills workshops are well attended, and there are multitudes of books on these topics. But there has been little focus specifically on counselling skills.

Counselling skills and techniques are simply a subset of interpersonal skills – a specific type of interpersonal skill. They are very useful in a wide variety of business situations such as problem solving, training and consulting. Recently the number of counselling skills courses being offered is increasing, and a higher percentage of the delegates attending are mainstream managers and supervisors, as well as personnel officers and 'helping' specialists.

The use of counselling skills was previously thought appropriate only for personnel officers or professional experts outside the company. Although referral is often necessary and appropriate, there are still vast benefits to be gained by managers from utilising counselling skills in specific managerial situations.

What are the benefits? Why would companies train managers in counselling skills? Don't you, as a manager, already have enough to do without becoming a counsellor as well? Your time *is* valuable, and using a counselling style of management can *initially* take more time and effort than a more traditional or directive style, but there are significant long-term payoffs.

NUMEROUS APPLICATIONS

The use of counselling skills makes good business sense! Counselling skills have direct application to many current trends, concerns and needs, for example:

- Change management:
  - An organisation's success now depends on its ability to adapt to continuous environmental changes (i.e. its ability to continually develop). There is less security for everyone. Change is much easier for employees to cope with if they feel a basic level of security at a personal level. This feeling is generated when an organisation genuinely cares about its employees, and assures that managers use counselling skills effectively to bring about a healthy climate.
- Quality initiatives.
- Performance management.
- Management development.
- Mentoring.
- Long-term thinking.
- Managing diversity.
- Equal opportunities.
- The learning organisation.

THE BOTTOM LINE

There is sound reasoning, both philanthropic and economic, for using counselling skills with employees. These skills can have a significant effect on corporate image as well as on the 'bottom line'.
  Philanthropic reasons include:

1. **Benevolence** Managing employees using a counselling style is a way of placing value on individuals, acknowledging that they are human and not machines or robots. Offering a more humane, positive, supportive and enjoyable work environment could be reason enough on its own for using counselling skills, given the large percentage of one's life which is spent at work.

2. **Motivation** Studies of work motivation have shown that employees are motivated as much by comfortable working relationships with others as they are by money. Of course this varies from person to person, but the importance of healthy, happy relationships as a motivator for high performance cannot be ignored.

3. **Personal growth** The benefits of counselling for the individual (coming to accept their feelings, learning to clarify and explore their options, and mobilising themselves to use their own resources to deal with problem situations) also become tremendous benefits to the organisation.

Given that the purpose of an business organisation is to make money, it is fortunate that there are also many practical and economic reasons for applying counselling skills:

1. **Maintaining company assets** Employees are an expensive company asset, and therefore need maintenance and caretaking just like valuable capital assets do in order to obtain most effective 'usage'. Managers who have the psychological techniques and skills to provide this employee maintenance will profit, because the benefits of counselling to the individual in turn increase the effectiveness and productivity of the employee and therefore the department and organisation.

2. **Lower absence rates** People often 'ring in sick' to relieve themselves of stress when problems become overwhelming. As the following statistics indicate, the cost of such absence is high. When given a resource to turn to, employees have been found to take advantage of the resource instead of taking time off.
   — Time off work with stress-related illnesses is estimated to have increased by 500 per cent since the mid 1950s, and now costs industry hundreds of millions of pounds a year. In 1991, working days lost through mental illness cost UK industry £6200 million (Department of Social Security).
   — In 1991, of the 517 million working days lost through sickness absence, 18 per cent (92 million) were due to mental illness. Half of all days lost through mental illness (45 million) were due to anxiety and stress conditions (Mental Health Foundation).

3. **Higher productivity/prevented underperformance** 'Presenteeism' (present but not performing well) is as much of a problem as absenteeism. Worried employees underperform. Counselling is a powerful resource for enabling employees to deal with problems with minimum disruption to their work.
   — In a survey conducted by Saville and Holdsworth Ltd,

occupational psychologists, 33 per cent of the general population sample responded that stress and personal problems significantly affected the tasks they performed.

4. **Employee self-reliance, development and effectiveness** A counselling style of management will empower employees to build confidence and independence, take initiative and develop their full potential. Knowing that support is available encourages employees to take the risks necessary for growth. The initial investment in time that using counselling skills takes pays off in the long run as subordinates become more self-reliant and therefore end up demanding less of their manager's time.

5. **Increased employee commitment, morale and loyalty** In return for the company's concern, employees will give back to the organisation in the form of high levels of commitment to organisational objectives and to their work. In the current competitive marketplace, the level of employee commitment can be crucial to a company's survival.

6. **Lower staff turnover** As a result of increased satisfaction with their relationships with managers, with their work and with the organisation as a whole, employees are less likely to leave.

7. **Improved corporate identity/public relations/recruitment** Word of mouth travels fast, especially regarding companies which take good care of their employees. Public relations improve, both inside and outside of the organisation, which leads to higher quality potential recruits.

8. **Monitored organisational health** Although confidentiality is obviously extremely important, statistics on the types of problems which are affecting employees can help the organisation to become aware of problem areas and to make decisions regarding action to be taken (programmes to be implemented, training to be delivered, policies to be reassessed, information to be disseminated, etc).

Given all the benefits, it may be hard to imagine why more companies have not already trained managers in counselling skills. The image of counselling in the workplace is rapidly improving, but even now some managers back away from the idea of counselling. They see it as a 'touchy-feely' activity which has no place at work. Attitudes towards the different types of helping are well illustrated by this quote from Ahern:

Coaching, mentoring and career management . . . are associated with high fliers, and are thought to be acceptable and positive. Coaching evokes macho sports images acceptable in boardrooms; mentoring connotes wisdom; and career management brings two popular corporate concepts together. Unfortunately, counselling can be seen to be needed only by ill-fated hapless individuals, when in actuality an employee stigmatized as stressed may be the only one facing up to the difficulties of an ineffectively run organisation.

A person who is able to admit that they have a problem (and we all have difficulties) and who is doing something about it should be recognised as having courage and strength.

There is a growing realisation that there can be a deeper and greater strength in acknowledging our vulnerability. To use counselling skills effectively it is necessary for managers themselves to attain a certain level of maturity and self-awareness, which can be frightening to those not wanting to look within. However, if this fear can be overcome the rewards to be reaped are great. Acceptance and understanding of the concept of counselling are growing as the benefits of using counselling skills within the workplace are becoming more and more recognised. Companies are beginning to realise that it is vital that the values and techniques of counselling are integrated into those of management and leadership.

2

Defining Counselling

I n order to apply counselling skills it is important to have an understanding of what 'pure' counselling is and how it works. There is general misinterpretation and confusion about what the word 'counselling' actually means. The definition is misunderstood because the word is commonly used in many different ways. If you ask people, 'What is counselling?', you will get a wide range of answers varying from advice giving (or even simply information provision) to psychotherapy. Figure 2.1 puts counselling in perspective relative to these other activities.

Counselling involves talking with someone about their problems and what he or she can do about them. It is not the same as the advisory role of a solicitor or an accountant. A professional counsellor will be supportive, but will not offer direct advice. Instead, a counsellor encourages clients to gain insight into their own problems, and helps them to become aware of and draw on their own resources. The process of counselling makes people feel more independent, more in control and more able to take action. Psychotherapy and counselling can overlap a great deal, but generally the term counselling is used when the time period is shorter and the focus is more on present problems and immediate needs; the

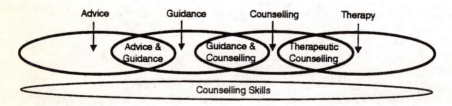

Figure 2.1   *The chain of activities*

Source: Advice, Guidance and Counselling Lead Body

term therapy describes an experience over a longer period of time where the distant past is explored in greater depth.

A DEFINITION OF COUNSELLING

Counselling is a process of interrelating which helps a person to:

- explore, express, and come to terms with their feelings;
- gain a clearer understanding of their motives, values and aspirations;
- draw on their own resources to cope more effectively.

In summary, the purpose of counselling is to help someone to help themselves. The concept of encouraging the individual to utilise their own resources, rather than attempting to solve problems for them, is key to counselling, and makes it different from other more directive modes of helping. Counselling emphasises taking action oneself, 'managing' problems and resourcing strengths, rather than finding solutions, fixing the problem, or changing someone else, because there are many problems which cannot be solved immediately and must be lived with (managed). Terminal illness is an obvious example; a difficult project team is a workplace example.

When applying the definition of counselling to the workplace, you need to take into account the difference between using counselling skills and 'pure' counselling. Organisational goals and pressures restrict managers from engaging in pure counselling.

'COUNSELLING' VERSUS 'APPLYING COUNSELLING SKILLS'

It is very important to make the distinction between the activity called 'counselling' and that of 'using counselling skills'. People often make the mistake of thinking that using counselling skills *is* real counselling. Although the words are often used interchangeably, it is important to keep the distinction clear in your mind.

The use of counselling skills entails more than effective listening skills, but is not by any means as sophisticated as the service offered by a professionally certified counsellor. The professional counselling process can be very specialised, and requires a great deal of fine-tuned expertise and experience. Your primary purpose in using counselling skills as a manager is to help your subordinates to perform in their functional roles as loan officer, consultant, supervisor, computer programmer, nurse, or whatever. You can very beneficially use counselling skills and techniques, but you cannot engage in a true counselling process, for two reasons:

1. **Role conflict** There are clashes between the objectives of the pure counselling process and the objectives of the manager. In a professional counselling relationship, the counsellor is employed by and working for the client. This counsellor is paid to be completely 'person'-centred, working solely for the good of the client. An employee and manager, however, are both employed by the company, and the employee works for the manager. The manager needs to focus on company and departmental objectives as well as people, and therefore often needs to move into the challenging and confronting phase of counselling earlier than a professional counsellor would.

2. **Lack of training** Professionally certified counsellors have a degree of expertise which goes far beyond the level of the basic counselling techniques used by effective managers. Someone who has mastered basic counselling skills but is not a certified counsellor by profession can only help in the most amateur way. Managers who acquire and use counselling skills will be able to listen, understand, communicate, help and motivate better than those who do not. However, it would be inappropriate to attempt to help with, for example, deep-seated or long-term emotional problems.

3

Managers Using Counselling Skills

EXERCISE 1 What are you managing?

Pick an average week or month of your work life in the past year. What percentage of your time during that period did you spend on making plans for the future? What percentage of your time did you spend producing (or servicing clients)? What percentage of your time did you spend on paperwork? What percentage of your time did you spend developing your subordinates?

Planning _____ %

Producing/Servicing Clients _____ %

Paperwork _____ %

Developing Subordinates _____ %

Employees, in their day to day work, need to recognise opportunities, deal with changes, resolve problems, prioritise and make decisions. As a manager, your effectiveness depends on their ability to do these things. If they are not doing these things effectively then you need to help them, and often it will be more appropriate and constructive to help them by using counselling skills than to use a more directive helping style.

Applying a counselling style allows you to help others with problems without taking on their problems for them. The problem remains with the owner, and, as much as possible, responsibility for the solution remains with the owner.

An encouraging result of a consistently adopted counselling management style is that you become highly respected and appreciated by your staff, and word spreads about your style.

MANAGEMENT STYLES

EXERCISE 2   Your present problem-solving style

Step 1. Think back to the last five times that you were asked for help by a subordinate. Write down a brief identification of the situations in the sections marked A below.

Step 2. Try to recall how you handled each situation. Write down what you did and how you did it in the sections marked B below.

Situations and your behaviours

1A. _____

1B. _____

_____

_____

_____

_____

2A. _____

2B. _____

_____

_____

_____

_____

3A. _____

3B. _____

_____

_____

_____

_____

4A. _____

4B. _____

_____

_____

_____

5A. _____

5B. _____

_____

_____

_____

_____

Counselling techniques fit in perfectly alongside the modern 'participative' theories of management style. The model of management styles in Figure 3.1 illustrates the continuum of management styles from most directive to most empowering.

- *Telling* is being directive about what you want to be done.
- *Telling and selling* is being directive, but additionally taking time to sell your decision.
- *Consulting* is telling your staff what must be done, but allowing them to help decide how it is done.
- *Joining* is deciding together with your staff what must be done in order to meet the objective as well as how it is to be done.
- *Delegating* is letting your staff decide how the objective will be met.

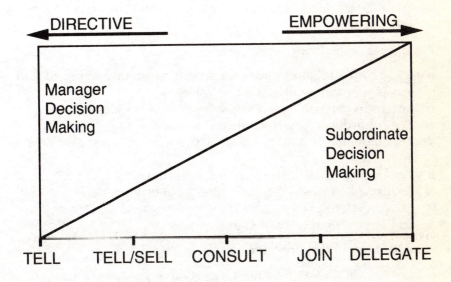

Figure 3.1 *Management styles*

Source: Adapted from Tannenbaum and Schmidt.

As a manager, you may have very specific ideas about how something ought to be done. The more that you let your staff determine how to go about meeting this objective for themselves, the more committed to meeting it they will be. You need to decide on the relative importance of having your own ideas implemented versus letting your staff come up with their own, or elect to compromise somewhere in the middle.

The benefits and risks of operating at each end of the continuum (directive vs. empowering) are summarised below.

Advantages of the Directive Style

- The solutions are the ones that the manager wants.
- The solutions are better ones and will be more accepted if the manager has the expertise.
- The subordinate is clear about the manager's expectations.
- Quicker progress and problem resolution (in the short term).
- Costs less (in the short term).
- Takes less energy (in the short term).
- The manager feels in control.

Disadvantages of the Directive Style

- Encourages subordinates' dependence.
- Brings about compliance, not commitment (less commitment to someone else's ideas and solutions).
- There may be existing unresolved issues.
- The manager can only raise problems to which he or she has solutions.

Advantages of the Empowering Style

- Higher level of subordinate commitment to, ownership of and excitement about decision or solution.
- Results in personal growth, development and independence.
- The subordinate understands the solutions.
- The solutions are better ones if the subordinate has the expertise/ knowledge.
- The manager may learn from the subordinate.
- Builds a good working relationship – subordinate feels involved, recognised, respected.
- Long-term benefits – saves time, money, effort.

Disadvantages of the Empowering Style

- The solutions/ideas may not be as good as the manager's.
- The subordinate may not have any ideas.
- Initial investment of time, money, energy.

- The subordinate may not view the problem in as broad a context as the manager.

Today's management theory advocates being on the right-hand side of the management styles diagram as much as possible in order to maintain maximum commitment from employees and harness the maximum resources they offer. Jargon used by managers trying to adopt a participative management style includes words like facilitating, empowering, ownership and commitment. Counselling skills are needed to achieve all of these effectively – counselling is the most empowering method of problem solving since counselling places the responsibility upon the subordinate as much as possible. The subordinate will consequently be more committed, and when he or she changes, these changes are more likely to be lasting, effective and pursued with enthusiasm.

When you decide to use an empowering style of management, this does not mean you can just take a totally hands-off approach, delegate willy-nilly and hope that all goes well. It is by no means an easy way out. Delegating and operating in a counselling style requires you to support and encourage employees' growth, which is hard work – but, in the long run, not as hard as having them dependent on you. The initial investment in time is worthwhile in the long term.

Obviously, you cannot do everything in a participative, facilitative and empowering manner. You must balance the needs of people and the requirements of business, and therefore need to be able to shift to different points on the continuum as warranted by the needs of the subordinate and the situation. Practical considerations and good human relations skills must be integrated.

Counselling skills can be integrated with other types of helping as needed. Coaching is more task or problem oriented than counselling. When coaching, you use your knowledge and experience to evaluate, advise and train. You listen and determine what the employee is doing right and wrong, and then tell, teach, or show them how to do it better. You attempt to get the employee to understand your reasoning. You might also give advice, suggest alternatives for solutions, and organise exercises and practice sessions. The coaching relationship contains differentials of power. Training requires a similar level of concern for achieving task objectives as coaching, but is less concerned with the individual than coaching. When training one tends to 'tell them how and leave them'.

When you counsel, your employees evaluate their own situations and behaviours. You listen, encourage expression of feelings, and encourage the employee to come up with possible ways of managing the problem. In a counselling situation, you and your subordinate are meeting as equals. You do not guide, but rather 'accompany' the subordinate. Using counselling skills gets to underlying root problems better than other types of helping because it allows subordinates to explore fully for themselves what is the real problem.

Blake and Mouton's Leadership Grid is also useful as a framework in analysing your own and others' management styles. The horizontal dimension of the grid measures concern for productivity or for the task to be accomplished – increasing efficiency and output standards. The vertical dimension measures concern for people and relationships – physical and psychological well-being.

- **9,1 style** Maximum concern for production. Minimum concern for people. Manager treats employees like machines, or simply as units in a production process. Scientific or authority/ obedience management.
- **1,9 style** Minimum concern for production. Maximum con-

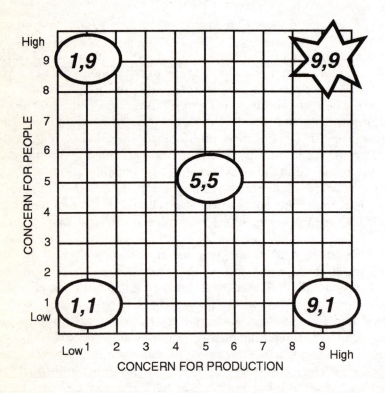

Figure 3.2 *The Managerial Grid*

Source: The Leadership Grid ® Figure from *Leadership Dilemmas – Group Solutions*, by Robert R. Blake and Anne Adams McCanse (formerly the Managerial Grid Figure by Robert R. Blake and Jane S. Mouton) Houston: Gulf Publishing Company, p. 29. Copyright © 1991, by Scientific Methods Inc. Reproduced by permission of the owners.

cern for people. Focus on human relations and comfort. Avoidance of conflict. Manager has happy employees who produce little. Country-club management.

- **1,1 style**   Minimum concern for production. Minimum concern for people. Minimum effort required to get by. Manager plays politics. Apathetic management.
- **5,5 style**   Compromise position. Balances people and productivity. Medium concern for both. Manager follows procedures and aims at producing the most without upsetting people. Not enough emphasis on people or on production to achieve 9,9 position. Mediocre management.
- **9,9 style**   The ideal. Obtains highest productivity through gaining utmost commitment. Production through people. Makes fullest use of all the energy in the system. Team management.

Many managers tend to operate too close to the 9,1 style, unaware or disbelieving that there is a more effective way. Probably even more managers operate in the 5,5 style where it feels fairly comfortable. Moving from 5,5 to 9,9 requires some extra special efforts, including using counselling skills with individual employees and with teams. Counselling in its pure sense is an activity in which the person is of the utmost importance and there is little or no concern for the task or company objectives – hence the (not surprising) alarm on the part of many managers when asked to consider adopting a counselling style. However, using counselling skills *sometimes* is one way of achieving the balance with the high concern for company objectives on the other side of the scale, which ultimately will bring about a 9,9 style of management.

ROLE CONFLICT

The previous chapter referred to role conflict. This is the real struggle for managers using counselling skills – the conflict with their roles. Counselling is easier for mentors or outside 'neutral' counsellors, who don't have as much riding on what the subordinate does and what choices the subordinate makes.

An employee is working for you and you must therefore assess and evaluate his or her performance and encourage him or her to behave in such a way that productivity is optimised. Do you then focus concern and attention on the task at hand or on the subordinate?

This task vs. people role conflict is always there for people in positions of authority and leadership. Good management is knowing when to focus on which. In many cases you will only help to improve work performance by dealing with the personal/people issues. But where do you draw the line? When does attempting to use counselling skills cross the line and move from being productive to being counterproductive to the organisation? Different managers will draw the line in different places. Many questions are raised over this long-standing debate regarding effective management, and it is very important for managers to think through these issues for themselves.

CHOOSING STYLES

If a subordinate has a problem at work, how do you decide which helping style to apply? Should you use your counselling skills, your coaching and advising skills, or should you just instruct them what to do? You need to be flexible and move to the different points on the continuum that different situations require. In many situations a mixture of styles will be necessary, and there are, of course, situations where applying a counselling style would be altogether inappropriate. As a manager, you need to continuously be aware of the different options, to make conscious choices between them, and then to apply the chosen option skilfully.

The counselling style is often the most difficult of the managerial styles for managers to master. The listening and empathy needed for the counselling approach are likely to be difficult to adopt. Managers are used to evaluating and decision making, and find it easier and quicker to give directive help. They generally feel comfortable (and important) when passing on information, giving advice, or taking over and solving problems on their own.

However, as there are many situations where the directive approach is ineffective, the ability firstly to recognise situations which call for using counselling skills, and secondly to apply the skills effectively is vital. It is also important to know when not to apply counselling skills (that is, to recognise when another managerial style is called for).

The style of helping offered will depend on four things: the situation, the subordinate's personality, the manager's personality, and the culture of the company. Below are examples of some situations where empowering styles are more likely to be effective and some where directive styles are more likely to be effective.

Empowering styles are more effective when:

■ You are quite sure the subordinate is capable of coming up with workable answers/solutions. It will be a more satisfying experience for them to feel highly involved in problem solving/decision making, and will be a learning experience for them.

- You don't care about the outcome as much. For example with personal problems, the subordinate could make whatever decision is best for them, but they need to make some decision because not doing so is affecting their work.
- A work problem is one that could be resolved in a number of ways, and you are not concerned about which way the subordinate resolves it.
- A decision needs to be made which will have more of an impact on the subordinate than on you.
- The subordinate has knowledge which will improve the quality of problem resolution or decision making.
- It is important that the subordinate has a high level of commitment to the outcome, for example whether to relocate or not.
- The long-term effects of not operating in a counselling mode could be damaging, for example post-trauma.
- You want to offer support, build the subordinate's confidence, or make them feel needed or important. For people in new roles, this can make the difference between success and failure.

Directive (task-oriented) styles are more effective when:

- The subordinate needs your contacts – does not have power or authority to do something themselves.
- The subordinate does not have the knowledge or capability necessary to solve a problem themselves.
- Time/cost limitations prevent you from using a more empowering style.
- The situation is a semi-emergency and fast action is needed.

Some general situations where a subordinate can be helped by your counselling techniques include:

- work performance problems;
- interpersonal difficulties;
- teamwork problems;
- transitions chosen by employee;
- unchosen employee transitions;
- opportunities for employees;
- effects of change;
- decision making;
- stress management;
- post-trauma or during crisis;
- personal problems (bereavement, divorce, financial worries, mid-life crisis, addictions, depression, etc).

It is useful to acquire an automatic procedure for quickly responding to standard situations calling for counselling skills.

Usually even more damaging than being too directive is being manipulative and pretending to be using counselling skills facilitatively when you are not. If your employees really understand the concept of counselling, they will correctly see you as manipulative. If they do not understand counselling, they may be temporarily fooled, but the long-term result will be at best confusion and at worst suspicion and mistrust. It is better to be honest and open about it when you want to be directive.

Many managers will say that they *are* presently using counselling skills with their employees as a natural part of their style and that all is going well. However, to quote Michael Reddy (1987), 'Counselling may be something people do naturally, like raising children or making love, but they do not necessarily do it well.' The skills need to be applied in appropriate situations and skilfully carried out in order to be beneficial and effective. Sometimes when people think they are helping, they do in fact make matters worse. Counselling requires more in-depth specialist skills than most people realise.

EXERCISE 3   Styles of helping

Referring to the examples described on page 9, think about which style you would apply to each problem situation given. There may not be enough information given in these examples to say what you would definitely do, as your choice of style will depend on the specifics of the situation and the person.

Problems such as the three described below will usually call for the use of counselling skills because the subordinate in all these cases knows far more about the situation than you do and is likely to be able to come up with some solutions of their own given a little support.

- A staff member approaches you because he is having difficulty getting along with a colleague on a project team.
- A subordinate tells you he is having relationship problems at home with his partner and doesn't know what to do.
- A designer on your team is losing her creative streak.

In contrast, the following problem is likely to call for a directive problem-solving method, instruction giving, because you as manager would know more about the procedures than your subordinate would.

■ You need to meet with one of your staff who has not followed the correct procedure for organising her holiday period.

Some problems will call for a mixture of styles to be used. Consider the following case:

■ You are receiving complaints from job candidates regarding the interviewing methods of one of your most successful supervisors.

Using a mixture of counselling skills and coaching or training would be appropriate here. This problem needs to be taken care of quickly as it is adversely affecting applicants and therefore also the reputation and image of the company. The supervisor is generally successful so it is possible that all that is needed is training in interviewing skills, but if counselling skills are used first, you can be more sure of your diagnosis.

Time pressures often push managers into going for quicker solutions (advising or coaching) which may temporarily relieve the situation, but often leave the real issues untouched.

■ An insurance broker trainee announces to you that he has missed the exam. Passing the exam is necessary to progress and to begin dealing with clients.

In the above situation a busy manager might be tempted simply to instruct the trainee on how to register for another test, but using counselling skills could reveal that there are further underlying issues which need to be resolved. The trainee might be worried about having chosen the wrong profession, or wondering whether he would be better off in a different division of the company. Overlooking underlying issues can be very costly to yourself and to the company in the long run, so it is often useful to use counselling skills first in order to help you determine where to go next.

In many circumstances, you will need to be directive and firm about an outcome or goal, and only allow for subordinate empowerment (input and decision making) regarding how that goal is to be brought about. So you may start with certain assumptions and objectives, and working from there adopt a counselling style. You need to be clear in your own mind beforehand how much decision making you want to do yourself versus how much you are *really* willing to delegate, and then you need to make this very clear to your subordinate as well.

CASE EXAMPLE 1

Sarah works as a manager for a foreign bank in London. She supervises two sections: office materials and supplies, and maintenance. When I met her, Sarah told me that she was sent to see me by her boss, Maria, in order to receive coaching in assertiveness skills. Maria thought that Sarah needed to learn to assert herself more with the three men who worked in maintenance.

As Sarah's description of her struggles with the maintenance department unfolded, it became obvious that she had been under enormous pressures and strain. I used counselling skills in order to help her 'tell her story' and help her express emotions of frustration and anger which she had been holding in for a long time.

She was extremely fed up with trying to get cooperation from the maintenance department, who were disgruntled due to feeling low-status and not having received a pay rise that year. They tended to take out their frustrations on Sarah by giving her a hard time in subtle, and some not so subtle, ways.

Sarah's present style of dealing with them tended to fluctuate back and forth from passive (avoidance) to aggressive (loud patronising lectures). However, as we talked I got the impression that she had the capability and know-how to be assertive, but for some reason was not doing so.

More discussion revealed that although Sarah had responsibility for the productivity of the members of the maintenance department, she had no control over their pay, nor their promotions. The authority to give 'rewards' was completely in Maria's hands, although Sarah performed the ongoing and annual appraisals. In such a situation, all the assertiveness in the world would probably not gain cooperation. Sarah needed to recognise the difficulty of her situation, stop blaming herself completely, and be more assertive with her own boss, Maria, regarding management structure, authority and responsibilities. Fortunately, Sarah recognised this quite quickly and was then able to move into problem solving – looking at the options for handling the situation.

We did do some roleplays to help Sarah get back into the habit of being assertive, both with her boss, Maria, and with the maintenance men, but this coaching represented only a small portion of my time spent with her. Using counselling skills enabled me both to understand the situation fully and to help her begin moving towards resolving it. Had I moved right into coaching Sarah, the real crux of the problem may not have come out, and I probably would have been very little help to her.

EXERCISE 4   Your present problem-solving style

Analyse each situation that you wrote down in Exercise 2. Using the management styles diagrams, try to determine which of the helping styles you adopted in each situation. What were the advantages and disadvantages of using that style? In any of the situations, would a different helping style have been more appropriate? Why? Write down your analyses in the spaces marked C below.

As you think about how you handled the situations, ask yourself the following questions:

■ Do I do more listening or talking when subordinates come to me with problems?
■ Do I want to take time out to really listen to people? Or do I try to find a quick fix to get rid of people with problems as quickly as possible?
■ Do I always want people to solve their own problems? Do I always want to solve people's problems for them? Or does what I do depend on the situation?
■ When I give advice or tell people what to do, is it to save time? To look clever? To look helpful? Do I feel as if I must have an answer to everything?
■ Do I feel a need to influence people to my point of view more often than is for the best?
■ Do I get to the real issues, or get to the bottom of what the subordinate's struggle is?

1C. _____
_____
_____
_____

2C. _____
_____
_____
_____

3C. _____
_____
_____
_____

4C. _____
_____
_____
_____

5C. _____
_____
_____
_____

WHEN DO EMPLOYEES BENEFIT FROM COUNSELLING?

Having established that it is necessary to be able to recognise situations which call for using counselling skills, there are two contexts in which a decision about management style is necessary. One is when a subordinate brings a problem to you. The other is when you have noticed something which may indicate a problem. How do you know when it is appropriate and advantageous to initiate counselling yourself? Below is a list of situations where a subordinate may benefit from counselling. (adapted from Reddy, 1987).

- They are not 'mobilising their energies':
  — not solving problems which they have the resources to solve;
  — not working at a level of which you know they are capable;
  — not making a necessary decision.
- Thinking is clouded.
- Unable to concentrate.
- Not responding to the usual motivators.
- Engaging in self-defeating behaviour.
- Unusually troubled, tense, anxious or irritable.
- Withdrawn from social interaction.
- Poor timekeeping.
- Increased absence.
- Lack of energy and enthusiasm.
- Noticeable unexplained change in behaviour.
- Problem pattern in behaviour:
  — falling asleep in afternoons;
  — drinking excessive alcohol during lunch;
  — decrease in performance level.
- Involuntary change occurs:
  — new boss;
  — redeployment.
- When others are disturbed by their behaviour.

CASE EXAMPLE 2

Allan, a manager in charge of a busy sales team, was very worried about a sudden change in one of his salespeople's behaviour. Stephen had always been a keen and energetic member of the team, but recently he had been leaving work early regularly and spending far more time in the private telephone room (a small room with a desk and telephone reserved for employees' personal calls). Stephen was still his cheerful, outgoing self with his clients, but seemed preoccupied when he was on his own.

Allan decided to approach Stephen to ask whether he could offer any assistance. He suggested they eat lunch together the next day. During lunch, Allan told Stephen that he did not want to pry, but he had noticed the changes and was concerned whether everything was all right. Stephen told Allan that he had been terribly worried recently because his eldest son had been suspended from school for selling drugs. When Allan asked how the family was coping with the situation, Stephen said that he and his wife were not allowing his son out of the house, and were trying to talk with him every evening, but that his son was very uncommunicative and would reveal nothing. Every evening they were met by hostile silence from their son, and Stephen and his wife were now arguing with one another.

Allan listened and acknowledged what a frightening and difficult situation Stephen was in. He asked whether the family had sought any outside help and Stephen said no. Allan suggested that Stephen could take some time that afternoon to contact some sources of help, and offered to get hold of a directory of social services which he had seen in the personnel department. Stephen seemed relieved to have a resource to turn to.

Fortunately, Stephen was receptive to Allan's assistance and suggestions. There was no guarantee that Stephen's family problems would be resolved soon, but by taking action early on Allan was giving Stephen the best chance possible, both with his family situation and with his work.

4

Managers' Apprehensions

MIND YOUR OWN BUSINESS

Subordinates will sometimes bring their personal problems to you. At other times you may encounter a situation where you suspect a problem and want to approach an employee, but feel reluctant to do so because it seems to be on a personal level, rather than strictly work related. In the first instance, managers often discourage subordinates by dismissing such problems as being out of the realm of managerial responsibility. In the second instance managers may fear invading privacy.

However, employees' personal problems *do* become an issue in the workplace because work effectiveness and productivity are affected. It makes sense to acknowledge this fact and to take steps to address personal problems without forcing or being nosy.

STIFF UPPER LIP

A common concern regarding dealing with problems in a counselling style is handling emotions that may arise. Traditional business norms have not allowed the expression of emotions in the workplace and it is not easy to undo this conditioning. Some employees, especially men, would feel that they had 'lost face' if they cried at work. Sometimes deciding whether or not to encourage someone to open up will be a dilemma. However, repressed emotions create blocks – blocks in productivity, blocks in creativity, and blocks in self-growth. The managers who overcome this conditioning and deal openly with problems as they arise, emotion and all, are the ones who will be able to obtain the utmost from employees.

HELP! OUT OF CONTROL!

You might have a fear that using counselling skills will unlock Pandora's box – that you will end up going too deep into someone's problems and then be unable to cope. With practice, you will learn to 'contain' the conversation – to set boundaries and limits for yourself. It is advisable simply to listen when you feel out of your depth. It is also important to know when and where to refer subordinates.

NO SEX PLEASE, WE'RE BRITISH

Do you have a fear of being embarrassed by listening to very personal problems, or of embarrassing your subordinates, especially if they are of the opposite sex? For example, some men would be uncomfortable discussing menstrual problems, while some women would be uncomfortable discussing prostate problems. However, discomfort can be acknowledged and/or referrals made.

DIGGING MYSELF DEEPER AND DEEPER

Many people fear making things worse by talking about them. In most cases, however, illuminating and discussing problems leads to action which makes things better, not worse.

MORE PROBLEMS? NO THANKS!

Operating in an open counselling style where there is more opportunity for problems to be aired can seem frightening, even stupid, to an already busy manager. However, problems withheld will quietly affect productivity and employee effectiveness, and often create much bigger problems in the long term. It is wishful thinking to hope that ignoring problems will make them go away – usually they get worse. The sooner the problem is dealt with, the less impact it will have on the workplace. But be aware that often things will in fact get worse *temporarily* before they get better.

JUST LET ME BURY MY HEAD

You may fear that the root of the problem will be something that you yourself would rather not deal with. The employee's difficulty could indicate a larger organisational issue which you will then feel obliged to address. Or you may feel uncomfortably obliged to 'rock the boat': for example, having to deal with complaints or allegations against a well-liked senior manager. But would it be productive in the long run for the company to ignore the issue?

GIVE ME AN ANSWER

Another reason managers are reluctant to deal with problems in a counselling style is that, because of traditional business thinking or conditioning, they think they must find solutions to the problems. Managers have usually been promoted on their ability to solve problems. They are supposed to be innovative in problem solving, not innovative in problem creating. It can be difficult to accept that it is sometimes beneficial to dig up submerged problems for which you don't have an immediate answer or solution.

More importantly, you do not necessarily need to find a solution or offer advice in order to help someone. You can usually help just by being an empathetic listener. This can often be one of the most difficult lessons for beginner counsellors to learn. They worry about not knowing what to say or do. Simply being there is sometimes the best thing you can do.

WHO, ME?!

You might be afraid that the problem is you. It may well be. However, it is still better to deal with it than to ignore it. You have the option of either addressing it yourself with your subordinate or referring them to personnel – whichever is deemed most appropriate. Although this discussion may be painful in the short term, if handled well it can avoid larger problems in the long term.

HOW DARE YOU TELL ME I NEED A SHRINK!

You will sometimes want to suggest to subordinates that they talk to a professional or specialist about a problem before it gets worse. You may fear a negative reaction to this suggestion on their part. You can discuss with your subordinates their attitudes towards seeing a professional, and reassure them that while their fears are typical, their conditioned attitudes could be preventing them from growing as well as from feeling better. Remind them that it takes courage to face up to a problem by seeking help.

UP, UP, AND AWAY

You might worry that the employee will develop themselves to the point where they decide to leave the job. However, most of the time having them leave is better than having them remain and be dissatisfied. Also, it needs to be mentioned that the nature of your organisation itself can deter you from using counselling skills to foster employee growth. A very justified fear which prevents managers from developing their employees is that development can lead them out of the manager's department and onward and upward. There is evidence that sometimes managers who are good at developing their subordinates hold themselves back. In order to avoid this, organisations need to look at how they appraise the performance of managers, and make sure that managers are rewarded, not punished, for developing employees.

PART TWO

The Counselling Process

The Process of Counselling

5-D MODEL OF THE COUNSELLING PROCESS

Many models of the counselling process have been devised. The 5-D model of counselling describes the process in five phases which are easy to remember because they all start with 'D':

1. **D**evelop relationship.
2. **D**efine problem.
3. **D**etermine goals.
4. **D**ecide plan of action.
5. **D**o follow-up.

The process of counselling is fluid. Phases do not necessarily follow strictly in the order given in the model. You will sometimes go back and forth between stages, and you might jump around.

Not all the phases are always necessary. Counselling could stop after any phase. Sometimes the first one or two phases are all that is needed. Having expressed the problem and then seen it more clearly, someone might make a decision immediately or come to a realisation, and not need any more help.

Counselling could also start anywhere in the process, although earlier phases will either already have been established or will have been quickly reconfirmed. For example, a subordinate might see the problem clearly and know what needs to be done, and yet be unable to act. In this situation you could start at phase 4.

THE PHASES OF COUNSELLING

Developing the relationship

During this initial stage you must create an appropriate atmosphere

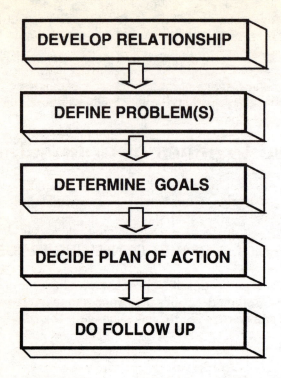

Figure 5.1 *The 5-D model of counselling*

and establish a special rapport with your subordinates. This 'safe' environment encourages them to open up more, to take a closer and more objective look at themselves, and ideally to challenge themselves in a way they might not otherwise do. The ability to self-criticise is a prerequisite to change and improvement. The conditions which induce people to open up in such a way are referred to as the proper counselling 'attitudes'. Carl Rogers, renowned for his 'client-centred counselling', emphasised the importance of the relationship between the counsellor and client in fostering client growth, and what he called the counsellor's 'unconditional positive regard' for the client.

In order to create the appropriate relationship there are 'attitudes' which have to be adopted in order for the counselling process to work:

1. **Respect** Respect for your subordinates is necessary for them to feel confident and gain the strength to move forward. Your belief in them is more important than your advice and knowledge in setting up a relationship which will encourage them to change for the better. It is important to make them feel worth listening to and to treat them as a unique individual, not a case

study. This means not jumping to conclusions, but trying to understand their thinking from *their* point of view.

2. **Genuineness**   Genuineness means being real (being yourself) and not putting on a fake professional facade. It also means being open and showing a real interest in the person. Pretending to be interested doesn't work. Falseness shows through and affects the relationship.

3. **Empathy**   Empathy is different from sympathy. It is caring about people and understanding them without also having to take their side, agree with them completely, or become overly involved. Responding to people in an empathetic way will encourage them to shift from talking about the problem in a general detached manner to talking in a more personal and emotional manner.

   Sometimes it can be difficult to remain distant enough from the problem if you relate to the problem personally. On the other hand, you can be too distant if you cannot relate to the problem at all. It is important to be aware of both extremes and maintain the right balance. Communicating empathy entails showing that you have heard, understood and accepted (not necessarily agreed with) what the other person has communicated.

4. **Equality**   An equal relationship is necessary for the process to work. A counselling session is a meeting between equal individuals instead of a meeting between a superior manager and an inferior subordinate. This 'meeting of equals' needs to be established early on and even more explicitly when using counselling skills in a work situation, since a manager does at other times behave more directively.

5. **Listening**   It should be established that you are there to listen to *them*. They will be doing most of the talking, especially in the early stages of the process. They will be leading the conversation – not you. This does not mean that you have no input or control whatsoever, or that you can sit back and take it easy. The kind of listening you will be doing is hard work, as will be explained further in Part III.

   You need to avoid changing the topic or taking the conversation in a new direction, except in cases when it is definitely necessary, such as when the subordinate is waffling, talking in circles, or not talking about what is really significant. In these cases it is best to point out to them what is happening and why you are changing the topic or the direction of the conversation. But generally you need to keep the focus on what is important to them, and let them lead the conversation.

6. **Confidentiality**   It is very important to set clear boundaries on

what will be kept confidential and what can not. Your subordinates will trust you more if they are clear regarding your confidentiality boundaries. Ideally, all your employees should have some awareness of this before coming to you. It should be stated as part of company policy. If you want or need to break confidentiality for some reason (for example, if you have obtained information which indicates that someone else may be in danger), this needs to be explained to the subordinate.

The effects of the relationship created by the above attitudes are that the subordinate gains confidence and independence, enabling them to begin tackling the problem. During this initial phase, they are often unloading, simply getting things off their chest. Talking about their feelings, thoughts and behaviours is a great relief. It clears their thinking and relieves tension and anxiety. When people think or worry about problems, their thoughts are vague. Amorphous, partially formed ideas, fears, hopes and images float around in their heads, often not in any logical or sensible order. Having to put them into words in a way which will make sense to someone else helps the person to begin to see the problem much more clearly.

Defining the problem(s)

During this phase, the problem is defined first by the subordinate from their point of view. The problem often then needs to be redefined more objectively before moving on towards resolution. It is important to show that you understand the problem from the subordinate's point of view *before* challenging them to look at the problem more objectively.

1. **Their view** You are seeking to define and understand the problem clearly from their frame of reference, and also to show acceptance of their view, even if you don't agree with it. Demonstration of understanding is achieved by using a skill called reflecting.
2. **Focusing and prioritising** You may need to encourage the person to talk about the most significant concerns, i.e. the ones having most effect on their lives. This may mean helping them to organise the issues. Often distressed people will throw a lot of confused talk at you, some related and some unrelated. In these cases you need to help them to sort out the issues.
3. **A new perspective** Your subordinate will frequently need to gain a more objective view of the problem situation before they can move on to finding productive ways of managing the problem. Often people will initially describe a problem as being

insoluble, or as being someone else's problem or the result of someone else's actions:

— 'There is nothing I can do about the situation. I am stuck. I have no control over company policy or management decisions so there is nothing I can do to remedy the situation.'

— 'She just doesn't like me. She is always trying to make my life difficult. She needs to learn to be more responsible.'

After having accepted and understood the subordinate's original point of view, you can then challenge them to look at the problem from different angles or to consider other points of view.

4. **Acceptance** The subordinate needs to come to the point of accepting that the problem does indeed exist before they will be motivated to do something about it. There is no point in using counselling skills with someone to help them to resolve a problem which they do not understand to be a problem.

5. **Ownership** After acceptance of the problem's existence, the subordinate's ownership of the problem, recognising it as being their own and not someone else's, is the next step. Ownership is a key concept in counselling, because it leads to self-responsibility. Ownership means acknowledging that the problem is affecting them, and is therefore theirs, so *they* need to decide what to do about it.

6. **Self-responsibility** A subordinate's dependency on you may have to be continuously but gently fought off, especially at first. Subordinates are likely to try to get you to give them answers. Get them to help themselves as much as possible. It is a good idea to talk about the dependency/self-responsibility issue openly. Keeping the problem analysis and solution generation in the hands of the problem-owners is the basic force behind effective counselling. They need to accept responsibility both for the problem and for doing something about it, which means they recognise that you are not going to take over the problem for them. When using counselling skills, do not allow yourself to be forced or tempted into producing quick and easy answers.

Consider the difference between the following two interactions:

Interaction 1

Manager:	'Right, that's the problem. What now?'
Subordinate:	'Well, uh, what do you think I should do about it?'
Manager:	'This is what you do. First you ... Then you ... and finally you ...'
Subordinate:	'All right. Thank you.'

After this interchange, the subordinate could leave feeling delighted that the problem is solved. However, the subordinate could possibly have other feelings about being told what to do. He or she could leave thinking 'That was a lot of use; I knew all that before I went in,' or 'That might be what they want, but I'm going to do it my way.'

In the following version of the interchange, the problem is put back where it belongs, with the problem-owner, so that they themselves work through from the problem to the solution as much as possible.

Interaction 2

Manager:	'Right, that's the problem. What now?'
Subordinate:	'Well, uh, what do you think I should do?'
Manager:	'You must have given some thought to the possible solutions. Have you any ideas yourself?'
Subordinate:	'I'm not sure, but one thing we might be able to do is . . .'
Manager:	'OK, that's one solution. Is that the only one or are there any other possible approaches?'
Subordinate:	'Well, I did think that perhaps . . .'
Manager:	'Good. Any others?'
Subordinate:	'No. I can't think of any more.'
Manager:	'We could always have a look at . . .'

Examples adapted from: *The Skills of Interviewing* (1988) by Leslie Rae.

Determining goal(s)

During this phase subordinates will establish their goals. They need to decide what they want to change, and they need to consider what can be 'solved' versus what can only be 'managed' differently.

1. **Choosing and prioritising goals and objectives** This topic will be discussed in more detail in the section on problem-solving skills. For now, suffice it to say that general goals need to be determined and then broken down into workable objectives. Objectives must be prioritised, and realistic time frames for meeting them considered. Some problems (such as an immediate difficulty with a client) are short term, and others (such as a desired change in career direction) are longer term.
2. **Commitment** The subordinate must be committed to the goal(s): otherwise, they are unlikely to carry out the plans decided on. The level of commitment and the need for it may need to be discussed rather than taken for granted.

Deciding the plan of action

For each objective, a specific and workable plan of action needs to be devised. To be workable, the plan must fit in with the subordinate's life plan, goals, values, and the time they have available.

1. **Generating and exploring alternatives** Subordinates may need encouragement or even help in exploring the range of options open to them. You might even need to remind them to consider that there are options, for example:

    —   'You have expressed concern about your relationship with the shipping department managers. What do you think can be done about it?'

    Subordinates may say they want to consider options, but don't know what options are open to them. You decide how much of your own assistance is appropriate. Suggestions can be made by you, or the subordinate can be offered a resource for finding alternatives (literature, another knowledgable person, etc), or you can continue to probe the subordinate for their own suggestions.

    Encourage them to consider *all* options, even ones they would rule out immediately, in order to examine *why* each is being dismissed. The reasons for ignoring or dismissing options can be significant. An alternative which is ruled out initially sometimes turns out to be the one eventually chosen. There is another reason for considering all the practical options available: it is useful to have fallback plans if the first option chosen does not work out.

2. **Decision making** Reluctance or difficulty in making a decision can be a barrier to moving forward. Methods for assisting your subordinate in learning decision-making skills are introduced in Part III.

3. **Specific steps** Once a decision has been made regarding the choice of option, then the strategy to be pursued needs to broken down into specific steps. Your subordinate may be tempted to jump into action with only a broad strategy to guide them, but the action is much more likely to be effective if each step is planned and considered carefully beforehand.

Doing the follow-up

The phase of counselling which is easiest to overlook is making sure that the action plan is implemented. Your subordinate will need to be taught, encouraged and reminded to manage monitoring (looking at indicators of progress), support provision and incentive provision for themselves. However, you can check with them at regular intervals to 'see how it's going', and can be available for back-up support, especially to help them to work through any blocks. In a work situation, depending on how directly the change is related to your objectives as a manager, you may want to arrange regular follow-up meetings in any case.

1. **All talk and no action**   Some of your subordinates may be a bit too comfortable in self-pity mode – complaining about a situation, but not doing anything about it. Throughout the counselling process, even during the first phase of empathetic listening, the manager must establish the expectation that the meetings are for working on problems rather than just talking about problems. Exceptions to this are serious personal problems such as the death of a spouse, where you are not qualified to help with the problem and can only offer an empathetic ear and/or referrals.

   Several precautions can be taken in order to facilitate action and to avoid the 'all talk, no action' syndrome. Opening the meeting with statements which set the expectations and time limits will assist in focusing the meeting. While the subordinate is determining the steps of their action plans, encourage them to think ahead regarding what resources will be needed, and what is going to impede the implementation of the action plans, and ways of lessening these impediments. Have them plan ahead for the provision of motivating incentives. Another source (or sources) of support may be necessary in cases where change is not going to be an easy process.

2. **Emotional blocks**   You may be tempted to encourage the subordinate to take action by 'pushing' them. Unfortunately, this is likely to make the subordinate more anxious and even less likely to take action. If the above procedures have been used and still the subordinate is not taking action, then it might be an emotional block which is preventing them from acting. You can use the counselling process to help them to recognise and overcome these blocks.

Below is a simplified example of a subordinate working through the five phases.

Phase 1 – Developing the Relationship

- Behaviours of colleagues described (they don't involve him in the decision-making process, he is being left out of the grapevine as well).
- Feelings discussed (anger, isolation, sadness, resentment).

Phase 2 – Defining the Problem

- As he sees it initially, others are excluding him.
- Continued discussion reveals that his workstation is physically isolated relative to his colleagues.
- It emerges that he may be contributing to the problem by not listening well and by being forgetful.
- Problem redefined as general communication difficulties.

Phase 3 – Determining Goals

- Find new ways to receive information which is being disseminated around the office.
- Improve his listening and remembering skills.
- Change workstation.

Phase 4 – Deciding Plan of Action

- He determines specific steps involved in devising and proposing a new system for memo distribution.
- He decides to request now a change of workstation next time someone leaves.
- He determines steps which need to be taken in order to obtain communication skills training for himself.

Phase 5 – Doing Follow-up

- He meets again with his manager a week later to discuss progress so far.
- Two weeks later, his manager approaches him to see whether his situation has improved.

Part II has discussed the phases of the process of counselling. You now have an understanding of how the process works and the appropriate attitudes required to create an atmosphere conducive to using counselling skills. It is the *combination* of the attitudes and skills which makes the counselling style of management work. Attitude alone is not enough; but applying the skills without the counselling attitudes won't work either. Part III covers the specific skills which have to be mastered.

PART THREE

Counselling Skills

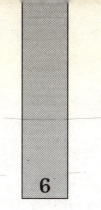

6

Listening

Listening is the *most* important skill for effective counselling. There are four basic types of things which you need to listen for when counselling subordinates (Egan, 1990):

1. Their experiences – What do they see as happening to them?
2. Their behaviours – What do they do or fail to do?
3. Their sentiments – What are their feelings and emotions?
4. Their points of view.

The special kind of active (as opposed to passive) listening which is exhibited by a counsellor has many positive effects:

- It builds rapport.
- It helps the subordinate to express themselves – even regarding issues not so welcome in the ordinary business environment, such as emotions.
- The subordinate feels you are there for them.
- The subordinate feels heard, understood and accepted.
- You will be more influential – listening builds trust. If your subordinate feels heard, they will in turn listen to you.
- It helps the subordinate to resolve their own problems.

In a counselling situation, you must focus on making sure that you have really heard what the subordinate has said, even when it is annoying or uncomfortable, and however much you disagree. You must also concentrate on the emotions involved and encourage the discussion of feelings – attempting to acknowledge the feelings rather than driving them away. This can be very difficult for managers who are not comfortable discussing feelings, or listening attentively to attitudes and opinions with which they disagree.

Most of us are not really very good listeners at all. Even though as adults we spend the largest percentage of our time listening, as school children we are taught a tremendous amount about reading and writing, a bit about speaking, and very little about listening. Given the lack of training, it is not surprising that our listening skills as a society are not very well developed.

The concept of active rather than passive listening is important because most people consider listening to be a passive, receiving activity. Real active listening is hard work and is very tiring because it requires an extremely high level of concentration. Unlike with reading, where you can go over a passage again and again, with listening you have only one chance.

Listening can be broken down into a variety of component skills:

- Reading body language.
- Listening to the *way* things are said (the sound of the voice and the words chosen).
- Being able to look through the conversational style and vocabulary in order to follow the thought that lies behind the words.
- Trying to understand values and way of thinking.
- Noticing what is not being said (due to hurt, embarrassment or guilt).
- Listening to the parts and the whole at the same time – learning to highlight the important things in one's own mind as the other person speaks, to think about how these might relate to one another, and to try to put them together to form a meaningful whole, or concept.
- Becoming familiar with the person's normal speech pattern so that you can discern anomalies which may indicate areas of importance.
- Practising self-discipline in order to eliminate distractions, overcome boredom, and concentrate on what is being said all the way through to the ends of the sentences.
- Demonstrating verbally and non-verbally that you are listening.

NON-VERBAL LISTENING

According to communication specialists, people communicate far more through posture, gestures and expressions (body language) and with the way the voice sounds than through the actual words.

Most people are not aware of how much they communicate to others through body language and tone of voice. Nor are they aware how much they are, often subconsciously, picking up from others non-verbal communication. For example, if you ask me whether I am excited about my new job, and I respond by looking at the ground, shifting my feet, and saying in a dull tone, 'Oh yes, I am

Table 6.1

Gestures/expressions	55%
Voice	38%
Words	7%
Total communication	100%

Source: Study by Albert Mehhrabian.

looking forward to it,' which would you believe – my words or my voice and body language? Most people would interpret me as *not* being thrilled about my new job, but not really wanting to say so.

In order to understand people best, we need to pay attention to all three components of their communication: body language, words and sound of voice. Because of its enormous impact, body language is very important. You will be able to communicate what you want to much more effectively if you are conscious of your own body language, and you will be able to increase your understanding of others (what they really think and feel) if you learn to interpret their body language.

It is useful to stop and think about how you would like someone to behave towards you if you approached them for help with a problem. Hqw would you like to be treated? Think about what a difference it makes when someone listens really attentively and encourages you, rather than someone who seems preoccupied, bored or in a hurry.

EXERCISE 4   Body Language Awareness

Think of times when you have felt that someone was listening very attentively to you and really cared about what you had to say. Make a list of the non-verbal behaviours that were portrayed which led you to believe that they were interested.

_____

_____

_____

_____

_____

_____

Next, think of times when you have felt that you were not receiving people's full attention. Made a list of behaviours which gave away their lack of interest.

_____

_____

_____

_____

_____

Body language

It is especially important to maintain attentive body language when you are using counselling techniques, in order to demonstrate attentiveness and communicate a positive, encouraging and caring attitude. Do not underestimate the positive effects of giving someone your complete, undivided attention. They will feel respected and worth listening to, which encourages them to open up and say more. They will also feel free to set the pace of the conversation and to take their time, which helps them to clarify their thinking.

Remember that talking to someone who seems not to be paying full attention has very negative effects. You feel small and unimportant, which may make you angry and/or upset. Your thinking becomes distracted and confused. You lose your train of thought and you may want to finish what you are saying as quickly as possible.

Below are the most important non-verbal indicators of attentiveness, or what counsellors refer to as 'total physical presence':

1. **Eye contact** Plenty of it, but not a stare. Shows interest, caring.
2. **Nodding** To acknowledge the speaker's words. Encourage them to continue. Nod at the ends of speaker's phrases, not on top of their speech.
3. **Facial expressions** Appropriate to what is being said. Shows that you are following along and empathising. Demonstrates interest.
4. **Open arm, hand and leg gestures** Physical openness demonstrates receptiveness, whereas closed gestures such as folded or crossed arms and legs demonstrate defensiveness or even insincerity. In fact, showing the palms frequently has been shown to make one appear more honest, whereas clasping the hands together and hiding the palms makes one appear less open and honest.
5. **Head tilt** Head slightly tilted to the side (like a dog does when listening) demonstrates interest and concentration.
6. **Slight forward lean** A lean too far forward can invade the other's personal space and appear aggressive or intrusive. On the other hand, leaning back can appear too casual. A slight forward lean, although not necessarily continuously maintained, is best for indicating attentiveness and alertness. Both lean and posture together can indicate your level of interest in helping your subordinate.
7. **Upright yet relaxed body posture** Sitting in a comfortable but attentive position communicates confidence and receptiveness. If you are relaxed, then it will be easier for your subordinate to

relax and open up. If you appear tense, it will inhibit your sub-ordinate.

8. **Note taking**   Often it is important to take notes for memory's sake, and doing so lets the other person know that they are being taken seriously. Note taking needs to be subtle, however, so as not to distract your subordinate's train of thought and not to break eye contact for too long. Avoid writing complete sentences. Instead, try to use your own shorthand.

Your body language should be sincere, so these mannerisms need to be blended in with your own personal style. You must be aware of the importance of these aspects of body language, and yet also be natural – be yourself. When these attentive behaviours are used insincerely and *ad nauseam*, they appear false and then have the opposite effect from that desired. Remember the last time you were annoyed while talking to someone who continually nodded, said uh-huh or mmm, and smiled too often and with all the wrong timing.

Body language which demonstrates inattentiveness includes:

- too little eye contact;
- wandering eyes;
- fidgeting (appears as if you have got something else on or at the back of your mind);
- yawning;
- frowning;
- total still silence;
- frequent blinking;
- looking at watch/clock;
- biting lip;
- slumped or rigid posture;
- hands in pockets (appears too casual, concealing, or arrogant);
- closed arm and leg gestures;
- tense;
- leaning/lolling back;
- leaning your head on your hand (appears bored or critical – best to keep hands away from face altogether).

A useful exercise for practising non-verbal listening is letting some-one else speak for a few minutes without saying anything, but showing your attentiveness through body language. The second part of the exercise consists of doing the opposite, showing non-listening through body language while they are speaking. Below is a list of the feelings and consequences which delegates on my courses have described occurring as a result of being listened to attentively and inattentively.

Being Listened to Attentively

- **Feelings**
  - Reassured.
  - Important.
  - Validated.
  - Worthwhile.
  - Special.
  - Cared about.
  - Relaxed.
  - Respected.
  - At ease.
  - Confident.
- **Consequences**
  - Trust.
  - Encouraged to talk more.
  - Open up.
  - More receptive to listener's comments.
  - Honesty.
  - Hope for future.
  - Feel free to take time and set pace.

Not Being Listened to Attentively

- **Feelings**
  - 'Small'.
  - Unimportant.
  - Stupid.
  - Upset.
  - Annoyed.
  - Angry.
  - Depressed.
  - Demotivated.
  - Confused.
  - Rejected.
  - Irritated.
  - Defensive.
  - Frustrated.
  - More fearful about talking.
- **Consequences**
  - Lose train of thought.
  - Speak incoherently.
  - Go blank.
  - Stop talking.
  - Defensive body language.

— Aggression.
— Energy and thoughts diverted to getting back their attention.

Because of the strong impact of attentive or inattentive body language, when using counselling techniques you must be sure that your body language displays full attentiveness.

EXERCISE 5   Your Body Language

Monitor your own body language while listening, first while not attempting to do anything new (in order to get to know your present listening body language). Make a note of behaviours you tend to exhibit to show listening, as well as undesired behaviours which make you appear not to be listening.

My listening body language:

_____

_____

_____

_____

_____

My non-listening body language:

_____

_____

_____

_____

_____

EXERCISE 6   Practising Body Language

With another person, practise 'listening' body language. An interesting exercise to try is to ask someone to speak to you for about 5 minutes. Tell them that you are practising attentive body language, and that you will not be saying anything, but will be demonstrating non-verbal listening.

For the first three minutes, demonstrate attentive body language, and for the last two minutes, purposely demonstrate inattentive body language. Observe what happens to the speaker as you are showing listening and then non-listening.

Afterwards discuss it with them. Ask them, 'Which behaviours made you feel listened to and which behaviours didn't?' Ask them, 'How did it feel to be listened to, and not to be listened to?'

Learning from subordinates' body language

You can learn a tremendous amount about your staff by becoming skilled at paying attention to their non-verbal communication as well as the content of the words they use. In fact, if you only pay attention to the verbal content of what is said, you may miss most of the message. The words are sometimes even hiding, rather than revealing, what is real. If you ask a subordinate who you suspect is struggling how she is, and she responds by saying, 'Oh fine, everything is moving along,' her tone of voice and body language are indications as to whether it is worthwhile probing further.

Some elements of body language which are particularly useful to watch for include:

- Eye contact – ability to look you in the eye. Darting or jumpy eyes. Glaring. Avoiding your gaze. Looking down or away. Blinking.
- Changes in appearance – clean to dirty. Neat to scruffy. Change in style of clothing. Can indicate health, self-image, state of mind.
- Facial expressions – do they match what is being said?
- Movements and gestures – what does the person do with their hands, head and feet? Still or moving about. Fast or slow moving. Smooth or awkward movements. Possible meanings of movements and gestures.
- Posture/lean – towards or away. Upright, slumped, or hunched over. Standing freely or supporting self on furniture.
- Satisfied/confident or not.
- Direction body is turned – facing you, or turned away. Do they really want to be there, or would they prefer to run away?
- General manner and bearing – withdrawn, nervous, aggressive, defensive, passive or not.
- Body language which often indicates lying or nervousness includes pulling on the collar, and putting the hand over or near mouth or nose.

It is important to look at groups of body language signs together, and not to make assumptions based on one indicator. It is easy to lose credibility by rigidly following oversimplistic body language rules. For example, having your arms and legs tightly crossed does not always indicate defensiveness. It could indicate coldness, or a need to use the toilet. The meaning of body language can also be culture dependent. Table 6.2 is a useful chart of some non-verbal cues.

Vocal messages

Vocal messages also give away a tremendous clue about true feelings. Often a change in the sound of someone's voice is telling, so knowing

Table 6.2

Non-Verbal Cue	Anger	Happiness	Sadness	Anxiety
Tone of Voice	Harsh	Warm Excited	Soft	Timid Hesitant
Voice Volume	Loud	Easy to hear Shouting for joy	Quiet	Quiet
Eye Contact	Direct	Direct	Averted	Averted Very intermittent

Facial Expression	Clenched
	  teeth
		Grinning
		Open
			Tearful
			Mouth turned
			  down
				Forced smile

Posture	Rigid	Relaxed	Slouched	Tense
Gestures	Fist clenched Finger pointing	Arms raised Jumping for joy	Holds head in hands	Finger tapping

Source: Nelson-Jones

their typical voice and noticing when they change from the norm can be useful. Some of the variations in voice include:

- Volume – loud or quiet.
- Pace – Slow or fast.
- Clarity – enunciation of words (affected or perfectionist, slurred or mumbled).
- Pitch – high or low, intense or relaxed.

Sometimes people's speech is totally muddled and incomprehensible, and therefore difficult to follow. However, the fact that the speech *is* muddled can, in itself, be valuable and telling information.

EXERCISE 7   Listening to non-verbal communication

Make a list of people's body language and/or vocal messages which give you additional or different messages than their spoken word. Think of times when you have learned more about someone from their body language or the sound of their voice, and times when someone's body language/vocal messages indicated to you that what they were saying was not the full truth. What were the specific behaviours which gave them away?

VERBAL LISTENING

By now you will be convinced of the importance of body language. It is also necessary to indicate verbally that you are listening to your subordinate. This section discusses several ways this can be done: using encouragers, echoing and key word repetition, reflecting, and summarising.

Encouragers

The most common way of verbally responding to someone in order to demonstrate listening is by the use of 'encouragers'. Encouragers are the short phrases and noises we make to tell people that we are listening, that we are interested, and that we want them to continue. Encouragers are minimal responses – enough to show that we are paying attention and not daydreaming, yet minimal so that we will only encourage, and not distract, the speaker.

If encouragers are too infrequent, the speaker will question our attention level. While using encouragers frequently is, of course, encouraging, overdoing it becomes artificial and distracting, and actually demonstrates non-listening. It sounds better to the speaker if we vary the encouragers we use, rather than repeating the same one over and over again, which becomes monotonous.

As with nodding (which is actually a non-verbal encourager), the timing of encouragers makes a difference as well. It is best to encourage at the end of a speaker's phrases, in response, rather than during or speaking over them, which is an interruption.

Following are some commonly used encouragers:

- Uh-huh.
- Mmm.
- I see.
- Right.
- That's interesting.
- Yes.

EXERCISE 8   Encouragers

Find a way to monitor your normal listening during a conversation (tape recorder, friendly observer, or self-monitor). Find out which encouragers you use and how often? Think about whether you could sound more attentive by using either more or less encouragers, or a wider variety of encouragers.

Echoing and key word repetition

As well as demonstrating listening, echoing and repeating key words are gentle ways of asking probing questions and directing the conversation. Echoing is simply repeating the last few words spoken, and key word repetition is picking out important words from statements and repeating them.

For example, if a subordinate says, 'Last year's European conference was not worth the trouble. The hotel was uncomfortable, the conference planners were disorganised, and we sent several salespeople leaving our office short-staffed. However, Roger doesn't agree with me.'

An example of echoing would be, 'Roger doesn't agree with you?'

An example of key-wording would be, 'The planners were disorganised?'

Both these examples indicate listening; they both encourage the subordinate to continue speaking; yet they both subtly direct the conversation as well.

Reflecting

As well as encouraging speakers to continue, verbal listening can communicate to them your understanding of what has been said. Reflecting is a way of showing understanding, without agreeing or disagreeing.

Part II talked about the importance of attitude when counselling. Reflecting is a way of showing non-judgemental understanding and acceptance, without becoming emotionally involved in the problem yourself. Reflecting demonstrates empathy and unconditional positive regard as well as listening.

So what exactly is reflecting? It is playing back to someone in your own words what they have communicated to you. The difference between reflecting and paraphrasing is that reflecting plays back the *total* message communicated to you (reflecting what you have learned from their words, the sound of their voice and their body language), whereas paraphrasing plays back just the verbal part of their message. In the example below Manager 1 is playing back the verbal content of what the subordinate has said, and Manager 2 is playing back the total communication.

Subordinate:	(looking downward) 'I have been asked to apply for that next grade position which was advertised. It looks interesting. (sounding unconvinced) Apparently I have all the qualifications necessary. I ought to apply.' (annoyed tone of voice)

Paraphrasing by Manager 1:	'You think you should apply for a position for which you have been specifically asked to apply due to your qualifications.'
Subordinate:	(looking downward) 'I have been asked to apply for that next grade position which was advertised. It looks interesting. (sounding unconvinced) Apparently I have all the qualifications necessary. I ought to apply.' (annoyed tone of voice)
Reflecting by Manager 2:	'You sound as if you are somewhat reluctant about applying for this position, but feel you ought to because it was requested.'

Reflecting total communication is often more helpful than reflecting only verbal communication. Manager 1 has understood what the subordinate said, but Manager 2 has given the subordinate some feedback, and offered an opportunity to explore the situation more deeply as well as showing understanding of what was said. The subordinate is more likely to feel better understood by Manager 2.

By choosing carefully which bits of subordinates' speech to reflect, you can direct conversations. This must be done with care because counselling conversations should generally be led by your subordinates. You can direct the conversation when it will help your subordinates to go in a direction which is important *to them*. This is different from taking control of the conversation for your own purposes. Manager 2 in the example above focused on the subordinate's reluctance because the subordinate's total communication indicated that may be important. Manager 2 is not manipulating the conversation in this case. Instead the subordinate is being encouraged to elaborate on an emotion which is obviously significant.

You can reflect emotion, thinking and/or behaviour. It is best to try to reflect as many of these as possible in a reflective statement when trying to communicate full understanding.

Supervisor:	'My head technician, James, has been doing steadily excellent work for some time now. He also trains the newer staff in a very positive manner, which boosts their morale at a critical

time. In order to keep him motivated, I need to do something more than just giving him praise, yet there is not another position between his and mine for him to aspire to.'

Manager: 'You have been rewarding James with good reviews, but you are concerned because you think something more may be needed to motivate him.'

The manager reflected the feeling (concern), the thinking (need for more motivation) and the behaviour (praise).

Sometimes it is useful to reflect back only the emotions which are not being communicated verbally, especially when the subordinate is avoiding discussing feelings. Thinking and behaviours are more often readily communicated verbally, whereas emotions are more often implied, or communicated non-verbally. For example, the statement 'I think I am being taken advantage of' implies anger, and an accompanying angry tone of voice or table thumping communicate anger. Reflection of feelings and emotions is a very important counselling skill because emotions are often a block to progress. Reflecting is a way of bringing emotions out into the open and discussing them, so that progress can then occur. Simple statements such as, 'You seem upset by this', 'You don't look so happy', or 'You seem quite worried' can help to get people talking about their emotions.

Time and time again my clients are sceptical about reflecting when I explain it to them, and express doubts about its usefulness: that is, until they either try it out, or watch someone else doing it well. Then they exclaim as they begin to appreciate its multiple benefits. Reflecting is an extremely useful skill which has many benefits for both the listener (reflector) and the speaker.

Benefits to Reflector (Manager/Listener)

- Demonstrates listening.
- Checks for understanding and builds clearer mental picture.
- Builds rapport.
- Paces conversation – gives you and them time to think about where to go next.
- Way of contributing to the conversation without leading it.
- Equalising – very useful for putting the problem back to them (avoiding taking on the problem and fixing it).
- Forces concentrated listening.
- Encourages opening up, going deeper – way of getting to emotions.

Benefits to Speaker (Subordinate)

- Helps to 'hear oneself' – therefore keep on track.
- Gains feedback about oneself – leading to better self-understanding.
- Feel listened to, validated, reassured and accepted.
- Feel understood, or have opportunity to correct listener if misunderstood.
- Hearing oneself more objectively through someone else – helps to put one's thinking in perspective.
- Clears and focuses thinking.
- Helps one to tell one's story.
- Allows one to set pace.
- Allows one to come up with own realisations/solutions.

People have very different conversational styles. Some of us reflect naturally in ordinary conversation. Others never reflect, instead tending to give other types of responses. Exercise 9 is a questionnaire devised to help you to recognise your ordinary, or natural, style.

Fill out the questionnaire choosing the responses to the statements that are closest to those you are likely to give in ordinary conversation (forget about the counselling situation temporarily while filling out this particular questionnaire).

EXERCISE 9   Typical Response Inventory

Based on the work of Carl Rogers, this inventory exercise is designed to find out what sort of responses you tend to give naturally in normal conversation. Read each statement and choose *one* of the five responses given which is *most* similar to the response you would be likely to give in everyday conversation.

Statement 1 (from man, aged 35 years):

'I have a lot of ambition. Every job I've had I've been successful at, and I intend to be successful here even if it means walking over a few people to do so. I'm going to prove myself and really go places.'

Choose one of the following responses:

A. 'You feel you are a very ambitious man, is that right?'
B. 'Why do you think you have such strong needs for success?'
C. 'That's good. You should soon get to the top with that attitude. Let me know if I can help you in any way.'
D. 'It seems to me that your needs for success are so strong that they outweigh your needs to be popular.'
E. 'It will make you very unpopular here if you maintain that attitude.

That's not how we do things here at all.'

Statement 2 (from woman, aged 26 years):

'Two years at business school have really equipped me to be a professional manager. Competing with men there has convinced me that women who get as far as I have are more than a match for most men. If this organisation wants to keep me they'll have to fit in with my own career progression.'

Choose one of the following responses:

A.   'A business school education is a great asset, but if you ask me it doesn't make you a good manager. You have to learn the hard way.'
B.   'What difficulties do you foresee in being female in this organisation?'
C.   'I'm sure you're right. We are really in need of people with your skills and drive. Let's get together next week and I'll help you plan out how you can get the experience you want in this department in the shortest possible time.'
D.   'If I'm hearing you correctly, you feel that you are well equipped as a professional manager and you expect the organisation to respect this?'
E.   'It appears to me that you have some worries about being accorded the status you think you deserve?'

Statement 3 (from man, aged 44):

'I used to be very ambitious but, as I've got older, success is not so important to me. I may not have been a success with the company, but I've put all my real effort into my family. I'm a very happy family man.'

Choose one of the following responses:

A.   'That sounds like a very sensible attitude, after all, very few people get to the top. Is there any help I can give you?'
B.   'Yes, you've reached the point where you decided to switch goals – from your career to your family – but you feel perhaps that something is missing?'
C.   'You're absolutely right. A man's a fool to keep struggling when nobody cares a damn. You did the right thing and I'd do the same in your position.'
D.   'As you have got older, you find more and more satisfaction with your family.'
E.   'Why do you feel that you weren't a success with the company? What do you mean by success?'

Statement 4 (from woman, aged 41):

'When I moved to this town I thought I'd make lots of new friends. Being single and living alone I've always had quite a social life. But it doesn't seem to happen somehow. The work is fine, but people here aren't interested in socialising much. I think it must be me. I'm getting more closed up and into myself.'

Choose one of the following responses:

A. 'Can you tell me more about how you go about making friends? Have you made any efforts recently to meet people?'
B. 'Living alone is all right if you have lots of friends, but without them it's very lonely – is that what you're saying?'
C. 'It looks as though you may be really worried about the future. Perhaps you've lived alone for so long that you've dropped out of the habit of getting close to people.'
D. 'That sounds really sad, to be lonely and without friends. What you've got to do is get out and about and make some. If I were you I'd get started straight away.'
E. 'Well, let's see. There are lots of ways in which you could get involved with the staff social club. Next month there's the annual outing and I could get you onto the organising team. What do you think about that?'

Statement 5 (from man, aged 32):

'I'm telling you, Lewis has really got his knife into me. I got the blame for the whole of the Brown and Williamson affair and there were eight of us involved. Now he's trying to insinuate that I'm falling down on the job. I had a good name in this office until he came here – he just doesn't like me and he's determined to bring me down.'

Choose one of the following responses:

A. 'You are getting paranoid feelings about Lewis. Could it be that you are working out your frustrations at not getting the job you both applied for?'
B. 'You're right, he can really be a mean so-and-so when he chooses to, but I wouldn't go about it with your attitude.'
C. 'Have there been any other occasions when he's tried to show you up in a poor light?'
D. 'If I understand you correctly, you feel persecuted by Lewis and think that he intends to ruin your reputation.'
E. 'Right, you need to protect yourself from situations like this. Do you know that the union is becoming very strong among our grades? In fact, I've got some application forms here which I can help you to fill out.'

Scoring

The scoring grid is organised with the situations 1–5 identified in the vertical column on the left, and response types identified in the top horizontal row. Moving row by row, circle your response letter for each situation. Next, add up the total number of responses circled in each column and put the totals in the bottom row.

You should now have scores for all five types of responses. The total of your totals should add up to 5.

E = Evaluative response – (making judgements).

I = Interpretive response – (reading between the lines, making hunches).

RESPONSES

	E	I	S	P	R
SITUATION 1	E	D	C	B	A
SITUATION 2	A	E	C	B	D
SITUATION 3	C	B	A	E	D
SITUATION 4	D	C	E	A	B
SITUATION 5	B	A	E	C	D
NUMBERS OF RESPONSES					

S = Supportive response – (sympathy, agreeing, backing up, offering psychological and physical support).

P = Probing response – (questioning, asking for more, often deeper information).

R = Understanding/reflecting response – (empathy, non-directive, non-evaluative response which reflects back to the speaker what was said).

Rogers' studies found that these five response categories accounted for 80 per cent of messages sent between people. Usage rankings were found to be: E – used most frequently, I – used next most, S – used third most, P – fourth most, R – used least.

In everyday conversation there is no right or wrong type of response. The appropriateness of different responses will depend on the situation. However, if you overuse or underuse certain types of responses, then your conversational style may be annoying, or even offensive, to others.

In a counselling situation, the most appropriate and useful response is R – which is the understanding or reflective response (although the other responses will sometimes be necessary). If you did not score any Rs on the inventory, then you may need ample practice to get used to making this kind of response.

Exercise adapted from Pedlar, Burgoyne and Boydell, *A Manager's Guide to Self-Development*, McGraw-Hill, 1986.

If you tend to give reflective/understanding responses in day-to-day conversation you will find it easiest to adapt to giving reflective responses when operating in a counselling style. If you tend to give evaluative or probing responses you may find it difficult to add reflecting to your repertoire of responses. Expect reflecting to be awkward, slow and hesitant at first. You will need to concentrate very hard in order to reflect accurately. Then you need to think about how to rephrase what you have just heard. Keep practising because it *will* become easier, quicker and more natural in time. Include it gradually in your style. You could try it out with friends and family before trying it out at work. Practise reflecting initially in a roleplay situation if it is very uncomfortable to you. Remember, if it seems difficult, it is because your mind is thinking about many things at once:

■ Concentrated listening – what exactly they are communicating.
■ Timing – when to respond.
■ How much of what you have heard to reflect.
■ How much to interpret without overinterpreting.
■ How to word your reflection without sounding like a parrot.
■ Not losing your own train of thought throughout the process.

A few words of caution regarding reflecting. First, avoid starting all your reflective statements with the same few words. This is a frequent mistake amongst beginning reflectors: 'So, you ...' is the most common. Used too many times in a row, the same initial phrase sounds very repetitive and superficial. Vary the ways that you reflect. Reflective responses can also be questions or statements. Below are some openers which can be useful for reflecting and checking understanding:

■ If I understand you correctly ...
■ It seems as if you feel ...
■ Do you feel ...
■ What I am hearing is that you ...
■ Am I correct in saying ...
■ So, you think that ...

Secondly, compose your reflective statements carefully so that they are not leading, manipulating or patronising. For example, a reflective statement which overinterprets and says 'so what you are *really* saying is ...' can be very irritating. You do not want to mandate how they are feeling or what they are saying. Instead you want to suggest how you think they might be feeling based on your interpretation of what they have communicated. Therefore, 'Do you feel...' is better than 'You must feel...'

And thirdly, do not use phrases such as 'I understand, but ...', 'I hear what you are saying', 'I know what you mean', in place of reflecting. These phrases may not convince subordinates that they have been understood properly because you have not shown *what* you have understood them to say.

EXERCISE 10   Recognising Reflective Responses

If you have completed the Typical Response Inventory (Exercise 9), you will have an indication of how you tend to respond to people in everyday conversations. This exercise gives you practice in recognising an empathetic reflective response.

Pick out the response which best reflects what the subordinate is communicating; in other words, circle the response which demonstrates most empathy and understanding of the subordinate's point of view. Also, try to identify which type of responses the other choices are. Compare your thoughts with the answers listed at the end of the chapter.

1.   Subordinate:

'I'm getting nervous because June is coming. If I don't pass the Series 7 test, I won't be able to move into the position of stockbroker, which is my reason for joining this firm in the first place.'

Responses:

a.   'This coming test is making you anxious because there is a lot riding on it.'
b.   'Don't worry. You will be fine. Just keep your nose in the books.'
c.   'You should have more belief in your abilities.'
d.   'You worry far too much. The test is not so difficult. If you are worried now, you are going to have a hard time as a broker. It is stressful work.'
e.   'Are you behind in your studies?'

2.   Subordinate:

'My supervisor is moving me into commercial sales now – just as I am beginning to excel in private sales. Will I never be allowed enough time to become successful in this organisation?'

Responses:

a.   'You should be pleased. Commercial sales is a wonderful opportunity!'
b.   'Why don't you like commercial sales?'
c.   'You feel you are being moved before you are ready?'
d.   'The commercial sales department has a very good record. You will have as much opportunity there as you do in private sales, if not more.'

3. *Subordinate:*

'Ever since I got out of hospital after the car accident, I've felt fragile and insecure. I can understand my feeling that way when I have to drive, but I don't understand why I am feeling it at work. How long is this going to last? People are going to lose faith in my capabilities.'

a. 'You are a strong person. It won't be long before you are back to normal.'
b. 'Have you talked to a doctor about this?'
c. 'People are seeing you as delicate, and treating you differently to before.'
d. 'Why don't we get together for a drink after work and see if we can cheer you up.'
e. 'You are concerned that your confidence in general seems to be shaken since your accident, and you wonder how much this will affect your work situation.'

EXERCISE 11   Generating Reflective Responses

Generate reflective comments in response to the statements below. Write your reflective responses on the lines below the statements. There is no one 'right' way to reflect but some suggestions are given at the end of the chapter.

1. *Subordinate's statement to Manager:*

'I can't contribute much to those project meetings. There is nothing additional I can offer when both Mary and I are present because Mary knows more about our department's involvement with that project. (sounding disappointed) The others must wonder why I even attend. But I need to hear first hand what happens in the meetings. They make such a difference to my understanding of how our work fits into the bigger picture.'

_____

_____

_____

_____

2. *Supervisor's statement to Manager:*

'I have been trying without success to get my staff to contribute their own ideas to our weekly meetings. I've given them the meeting agenda beforehand so they can think ahead about the topics. I've told them time and time again that I want their involvement. But they clam up as soon as the meetings begin. I find myself having to do all the talking. It's like pulling teeth to get them to elaborate on responses to my questions and ideas.'

_____

_____

_____

_____

3. *Account Manager's statement to Colleague:*

'My boss never listens to me. It doesn't matter whether I put forth my suggestion in writing as a memo, or verbally in a meeting, or even over lunch. She always nods and says she'll think about what I say, but then she never *does* anything.'

_____

_____

_____

_____

4. *Employee's statement to Personnel Officer:*

'This company is not what it claims to be! All this talk about caring and about developing staff. I am so overworked, and my manager never asks me to stay late – he just tells me! And, I still have not been able to attend that training course I was promised.'

_____

_____

_____

_____

5. *Salesperson's statement to Regional Sales Manager:*

'Since my wife left me I have been depressed. I don't think I deserve this. I always worked so hard to support my family, and now my sales figures are slipping.'

_____

_____

_____

_____

EXERCISE 12   Practising Reflecting

You can practise responding with empathy in a roleplay or in everyday conversations. If your score for R (reflecting/understanding response) on the Typical Response Inventory was 2 or higher, then practising reflecting probably will not be very difficult for you. But if you naturally tend to use a lot of evaluative or probing responses, then learning to use reflective responses might be awkward and difficult at first. Practise reflecting first in roleplay situations, and then during conversations at home or with friends, before trying it out on subordinates. At first you will be slow, hesitant, and you may lose your train of thought. Once you get used to it, though, you will see how beneficial reflecting is.

Remember to:

- Use 'you' or 'your' where they have used 'I', 'me', 'my'.
- Reflect feeling as well as content.
- It is often useful to reflect the feeling and then the reason for the feeling: 'You feel ... because ...'
- You do not need to reflect everything they say. Try to reflect the main message(s) being communicated.

Summarising

When using counselling techniques with a subordinate, it is very useful to summarise at certain points during the conversation. Summarising is different from reflecting. Reflecting is playing back what the subordinate has communicated in their last statement or paragraph. Summarising is concisely listing and/or tying together the main points covered so far during the session, or during a large portion of the session.

Like reflecting, summarising makes your subordinates feel listened to, and helps them to organise things in their minds. It also gives them an overview of what they have covered, and allows them the opportunity to assimilate and contemplate the discussion with a better perspective. This can help them to decide where next to direct the conversation.

Subordinates may throw a lot of confused talk at you, some related and some unrelated to their main concern. In these cases, you need to help them sort out the issues. One way to do this is to summarise the issues which have been mentioned and then ask them which one(s) they think should be dealt with first.

For example:

Subordinate: 'The new machinery that has been purchased does not have some of the necessary features that the old equipment had. I am the only person who has been trained properly to use it... My newest operator doesn't seem to fit in with the team at all... The busy season is arriving quickly and customers are really pushing us. I don't know what to tell them ... I don't have enough time for all this.'

Manager: 'You have brought up several problems: the capability of the new equipment we've purchased, the training of the users, managing your new operator, the busy season and customer requests, and your lack of time. Which do you think needs to be addressed first?'

Summarising will often help your subordinate pull together their thoughts and proceed in a meaningful way, and can stimulate them to move on the next step in the process – either looking into the situation more deeply, recognising repeating patterns in themselves, looking at the situation from a new perspective, or deciding on a goal or plan of action. Summarising can also be used as a transitional way for you to move the conversation on when you feel a need for some of your own input.

Manager: 'You've indicated concerns in several areas. First of all, your bookkeepers are making more mistakes than usual, you feel pressured by your colleagues, and you are tired and feeling physically unwell. I'd like to comment on ... because...'

Another helpful time to summarise is when your subordinate dries up. If they have gone blank, lost their train of thought, or become confused, the summary is likely to help them to pull together their thoughts and proceed in a meaningful way.

It is essential to summarise at the end of a counselling session. If the meeting is one of a series, then it is helpful to begin follow-up meetings by summarising the last meeting. Summarising intermittently throughout the interview is also beneficial, especially at points where the subordinate seems stuck and unsure how to move on.

VERBAL NON-LISTENING

Because encouraging, reflecting and summarising are such powerful prompters, often they are all the response that is needed during the first phase of the counselling process. Unfortunately everyone has some conversational habits which are not at all encouraging, and although these are necessary in some cases, they need to be avoided when using counselling techniques.

Such 'conversation stoppers' are things that we say in everyday conversation when we do not really want to listen to someone. Some are habits which we have adopted to protect ourselves from having to hear others complaining. Others are simply comments which tend to cut off the conversation, rather than encouraging the person to go into more depth.

In some work environments, these are the only types of responses that employees get when they approach a manager with a problem. Staff who take the trouble to approach others for help are often the most motivated and responsible, and it is unfortunate that they should be discouraged by receiving a conversation-stopping remark in return.

Managers who use these conversation-stopping devices are usually not aware that what they are doing can be harmful. They may be missing signals that more help is called for, or they may even think that they *are* helping. These managers do not realise the potential negative effects of verbally brushing things under the carpet.

The following are ways of communicating to people that we do not really want them to continue. They are not helpful when counselling.

Leading/directing the conversation

Notice the difference between Manager 1's and Manager 2's responses in the exchanges below:

Salesperson:	'I'm worried about my relationship with the clients.'
Manager 1:	'Which clients in particular concern you?'
Salesperson:	'Client X and Client Y are the ones I am most worried about.'
Manager 1:	'Why those two more than the others?'
Salesperson:	'Because they are the largest sales volume clients for our latest software package.'
Salesperson:	'I'm worried about my relationship with the clients.'
Manager 2:	'You are worried?'
Salesperson:	'Yes, I dread having to tell them about the bug I have discovered in the new software package. They won't be pleased.'
Manager 2:	'You are dreading their reaction to the news? What concerns you most?'

Salesperson: 'I'm not sure what the best way is to break the news to them.'

Manager 1 led the conversation too much and ended up going down the wrong track. Manager 2 reflected and asked open questions which encouraged the salesperson to talk about their concerns. This way Manager 2 was able to get the bottom of the salesperson's problem, which was finding the best way to broach the subject of the bug with the clients.

Reflecting and asking general open questions that encourage the other person to lead is the way to avoid this.

Blaming

'It's your own fault you know. You ignore everything he says at meetings. No wonder he won't cooperate with you on the project.'

If you think they *are* to blame, there is not much point in telling them in this blaming manner. You are likely to get a defensive reaction. More appropriate ways of challenging behaviour will be discussed in the chapter on challenging and confronting.

'It's all in your head'

Telling people that a problem is all in their mind makes matters worse. Their reality is real for them and although they may be imagining some things, there are probably good reasons why they have these imaginings and feelings. In phase 1, accept their reality as they see it. Then, when they seem ready for the challenging phase, you can consider together how much of their problems are created by themselves.

Interrogating

Probing question after probing question can seem invasive and accusatory.

Playing 'psychiatrist'

'You are a bit neurotic. This is why you are so obsessively perfectionist about these reports.'

Managers generally do not have the psychological expertise to label people, and they will be resented for doing so. Putting up an expert front will create a barrier and can do more harm.

Twisting their words

Subordinate: 'I don't think this department is running well. The A and B departments are much better organised.'

> *Manager:*   'So you're saying you don't want to work with us any more.'

Sarcasm

Cynical or sarcastic comments create blocks and are always inappropriate to an encouraging atmosphere. These remarks make others feel defensive, or teased.

Cheering up/humouring

'You'll be OK. Let's go and have a drink.'
'Hang in there. It'll pass with time.'
'Don't worry.'

These statements are pushing away the distress. They prematurely attempt to make the person feel better. Many people genuinely think they are helping when they do this, but they are not. Brushing aside the negative feelings is the same as dismissing the problem.

Not accepting feelings, not allowing negative feelings

'You shouldn't feel angry about it. You should be grateful.'
'Everyone goes through these sorts of things.'

Advice giving

'This is what you need to do ...'

In some cases this is a necessary response, but it will not help the person to be able to solve their own problem(s). It stops them from talking and working out their own solution, and instead makes them dependent on you.

Leading statements

'Can't you see that ...?'
'Don't you want to be promoted?'

These kind of statements are leading questions. They are not encouraging an honest exploration, they are directives hidden as questions.

LISTENING BARRIERS

Be aware of what is going on in your own head while you are listening. The following are some barriers to listening to look out for.

Fear of listening too well

Are you afraid to really listen? Do you fear losing your own train of thought if you listen too well? Or do you fear that your opinion will be changed by listening? You may worry that if you do not jump in to disagree you will be seen to be agreeing. All these fears are unfounded. If you lose your train of thought, it will be temporary. If your opinion is changed, maybe the other person's ideas are better. And there will always be time later on, after listening, to disagree.

Listening for what you want to hear

If you are a very poor listener you hear what you want to hear rather than what is being said. This has a disastrous effect on relationships with subordinates.

Personal limitations which affect interpretation

Your basic assumptions can affect what you hear. These assumptions are based on your personal experiences and memories, perceptions, values, biases, attitudes, expectations and feelings.

Emotional reactions

Sometimes people react strongly to certain words or phrases which happen to evoke emotional responses. This interferes with their ability to hear what is said after the emotive words.

Lack of self-awareness

Lack of awareness of your own feelings and struggles makes it difficult to listen to other people's.

Thinking ahead

Words are spoken at a rate of approximately 150 per minute, but the brain can process information about three times as fast. When counselling it is inappropriate to use this spare thinking time for planning your own next words or thinking about something else, as you might during ordinary conversation. Concentrated listening means listening all the way to the ends of sentences and using spare time to think about what the other person is communicating.

Self-consciousness

If you are worried about how you appear or nervous about what you are going to say next, your listening will be distracted.

EXERCISE 13   Listening Self-Awareness

This questionnaire has been devised in order to help you to understand yourself better as a listener. Self-understanding is an important factor in self-improvement. Answer the following questions as honestly as you can.

What makes me want to listen to someone?

_____

_____

What makes me feel good about the person I am listening to?

_____

_____

_____

What makes me feel negatively towards them?

_____

_____

_____

What do people do that makes me feel comfortable when listening to them?

_____

_____

_____

What do people do that makes me respect them when I am listening to them?

_____

_____

_____

What do they do that loses my respect?

_____

_____

_____

What things do people do that distract me when I am listening to them?

_____

_____

_____

What mannerisms do I find annoying when listening?

_____

_____

_____

What makes me lose interest in a person who is speaking?

_____

_____

_____

What subjects do I feel uncomfortable listening to?

_____

_____

_____

Am I often in a hurry when listening?

_____

_____

_____

Am I running on mental overload most of the time?

_____

_____

_____

Am I distracted by what is going on around me?

_____

_____

_____

Do I feel self-conscious when listening?

_____

_____

_____

Am I often thinking about what I am going to say next?

_____

_____

_____

Do I often think that I already know what the speaker is going to say ahead of time?

_____

_____

_____

Am I often tired when listening? Do I use listening time to rest?

_____

_____

_____

Am I often confused by the topic or the speaker?

_____

_____

_____

Do I often daydream while listening?

_____

_____

_____

Do I worry about other things while listening?

_____

_____

_____

What do I tend to think about when I am listening to someone?

_____

_____

_____

What listening problems do I have?

_____

_____

_____

How could I be a better listener?

_____

_____

_____

SUMMARY OF LISTENING TIPS

- Stop talking. Give yourself the space and the time to be really there for your subordinate.
- Concentrate. Focus on what is happening and try not to be distracted.
- Check for understanding frequently by reflecting.
- Watch the subordinate's body language.
- Listen to *how* things are said.
- Listen for what is *not* said – what is being avoided.
- Recognise your responses and try to put your own feelings aside. Are you switching off? mentally arguing? overidentifying? stereotyping?
- Be aware of your own body language (use the SOLER acronym to help you remember):
    Sit squarely.
    Open gestures.
    Lean slightly forward.
    Eye contact.
    Relax.

EXERCISE 10   Answers

1.a. Empathetic, reflective.
  b. Patronising, dismissive of emotions.
  c. Directive, patronising, judgemental.
  d. Judgemental.
  e. Probing.

2.a. Judgemental, dismissive.
  b. Probing, overinterpretive.
  c. Empathetic, reflective.
  d. Dismissive, leading, evaluative.

3.a. Evaluative.
  b. Probing.
  c. Overinterpretive.
  d. Dismissive, trivialising.
  e. Empathetic, reflective.

EXERCISE 11   Reflections

1. 'You feel in a bind because although you don't want to appear "useless" at the meetings, you are in need of the information you gain from them.'
2. 'So now you feel frustrated because your efforts to get more staff involvement in your meetings have not made a difference.'
3. 'You have tried very hard to be heard by your boss, but to no avail. You seem frustrated/fed up/angry.' (Depending on the asso-

ciated body language any of the above three feelings could be construed.)

4. 'You feel angry because you think that the company is all talk, no action, when it comes to concern for its employees.'

5. 'You are sorry for yourself because even though you tried hard to provide for your family your marriage still didn't work out. Now you feel as if your motivation for working hard has disappeared.'

7

Questioning

Questions are asked for many purposes when using counselling techniques with employees. Different types of questions will be asked in varying frequencies depending on which phase of the counselling process you are in. Some reasons for asking questions are listed below.

THE PURPOSES OF QUESTIONS

1. **Demonstrating interest** Asking an appropriate and intelligent question is a way of showing that you are listening.
2. **Clarifying** Clarifying questions help to clear up any confusion, giving you a clearer big picture.
3. **Probing** A focusing question encourages elaboration on areas you think may be significant for the subordinate.
4. **Checking facts** This type of question should only be asked when it is necessary to have a clear understanding of the situation. Don't divert the conversation with unnecessary fact checking.
5. **Eliciting personal reactions** At work people tend to speak on a logical level, leaving out emotions. Questions regarding feelings will give the subordinate permission to talk on an emotional level. Psychologists are famous for the question 'How do you feel about that?'
6. **Testing interpretations, understanding and conclusions** A reflective question asks whether your interpretation of what the other person has said is accurate.
7. **Challenging** Questioning is the most useful form of challenging.
8. **Making suggestions** Questioning is a subtle way of putting forward your own suggestions (without being too directive).

It is *not* appropriate to ask questions simply out of curiosity. Satisfying your curiosity may be tempting, but it won't help to create an atmosphere conducive to opening up and solving problems. If the questions are not leading somewhere which helps the subordinate to look into or resolve the problem, they may pick up on this and feel uncomfortable.

TYPES OF QUESTIONS

Open questions

Open questions elicit a long response or explanation. They are useful for getting people talking, probing, eliciting personal reactions, challenging, and making suggestions. These questions often start with words such as 'How', 'Tell me about', 'Why', and 'What'. Examples of open questions are, 'Why do you think that is so?', 'How did you deal with the situation?', 'What alternatives do you have?'

The responses to open questions tell you more about the respondent than those to closed questions do, because open questions do not place limitations on or lead the response. Note the difference between the open and closed questions below:

- *Closed:* 'Did you think yesterday's meeting was effective?'
- *Open:* 'What did you think of yesterday's meeting?'

The closed question is likely to invoke a 'yes' or 'no' as an answer. From this you learn whether or not the other person thought the meeting was effective, but you do not learn about the thinking or reasoning behind their answer. You do not know *why* they thought the meeting was effective or ineffective. The second question is more likely to elicit a response which explains why they thought the meeting was effective or not. Also the response to the second questions is more likely to tell you what is important to this particular person. They might mention the politics of the meeting, or whether it ran over time, or whether or not a conclusion was reached.

Some managers are averse to using open questions because they feel uncomfortably out of control of the conversation. However, when you are using counselling techniques you want to get the other person talking, so asking a question which encourages them to take the floor for a while is a positive move.

Closed questions

Closed questions generate short answers – questions which have yes/ no answers such as 'Did you attend the plant safety training course?', or questions which have simple, quick answers such as 'How old are you?' or 'Which department do you work in?' Closed questions are useful for clarifying or for checking facts and for getting people to be more precise and specific in what they are saying.

Some people have a habit of asking too many closed questions, and they often do not understand why they have difficulty getting and keeping conversations going. Many times people ask closed questions which would receive a more useful response if they were asked as open questions, as illustrated in the examples below.

Probing questions

Probing questions are questions leading on from or going deeper into what the person has previously said. They can be either open or closed. A probing question or remark invites the person to discuss an issue more fully.

Example:

- Closed question: 'Do you like the new telephone system?'
- Response: 'No.'

- Open question: 'Tell me about the problems that you are having.'
- Response: 'It is more trouble than the old system we had. Everyone is struggling with using it. It is questionable whether the investment will pay off.'

- Probing/open question: 'Why do you think people are finding it difficult to use?'

- Probing/closed question: 'Would you struggle less if you received more training on it?'

Table 7.1

Closed Questions	Open Questions
Did your promotion improve your situation?	How has your promotion affected you?
Have you talked to your staff about the project results?	How did you handle your staff regarding the project results?
Are you excited?	How do you feel?
Do you approve of the way the programme is being run?	What do you think about the way the programme is being run?
Do you get along with your colleagues?	Tell me about how you are getting along with your colleagues.

Probing questions are useful for obtaining more details, clarifying, eliciting feelings, comprehending the thinking behind actions, and encouraging elaboration on issues brought up tentatively.

Only ask probing questions if they are relevant to the subordinate's problem. Do not ask just for the sake of filling up a space in the conversation. Silence is much better than a useless question.

Continuous probing sounds interrogational and can direct the conversation too much. Probing needs to be interspersed with empathetic responses and open questions which do not direct the conversation, but instead allow time and space for the subordinate to lead the discussion and to go deeper into the 'real' problem. Notice the difference between the managers' responses below.

Subordinate:	'I'm afraid I won't be able to handle this new position.'
Manager 1:	'Which bit can't you handle?'
Subordinate:	'It's the demanding clients.'
Manager 1:	'Which clients are demanding?'
Subordinate:	'The M&G Company and BDZ Ltd are the most difficult.'
Manager 1:	'Why are they difficult?'

These are very common responses in everyday communication style. But look what happens when more empathy and less directive questions are used:

Subordinate:	'I'm afraid I won't be able to handle this new position.'
Manager 2:	'Can you tell me a bit more about your fears?'
Subordinate:	'Some of the clients are demanding. When I get pressured by them, I lose my composure.'
Manager 2:	'Do you feel you can't cope under pressure?'
Subordinate:	'I just lose my ability to think straight when I am pushed or harried by others.'
Manager 2:	'So you are having difficulty concentrating when clients pressure you.'
Subordinate:	'Yes, I don't know if there is anything I can do about this.'

It is important to move forward slowly and carefully. Do not jump into a problem area too quickly. Wait to let the full picture emerge before focusing down the conversation.

When probing, be careful about using 'why?'. It can sound critical.

EXERCISE 14   Question Types

This is an exercise to help you to determine which question types you naturally tend to use more or less of.

You need two people to work with you: one to converse with you, and one to record the kinds of questions you use in the designated chart below.

The chart is designed so that the recorder can record the types of questions used in the chronological order in which they are asked, by making ticks, moving from the left to the right over the time period covered (5–10 minutes suggested). When a probing question is asked, the recorder will need to tick twice to designate whether the probing question is open or closed. See examples below.

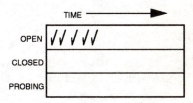

Figure 7.1   *Example of someone who asks many open questions*

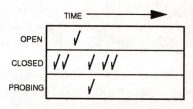

Figure 7.2   *Someone who asks many closed questions*

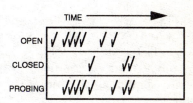

Figure 7.3   *Someone who asks many probing questions*

Pick a topic which is conducive to asking questions, for example the person's job, or their last holiday. Ask the person who will be talking with you only to answer questions which they are asked.

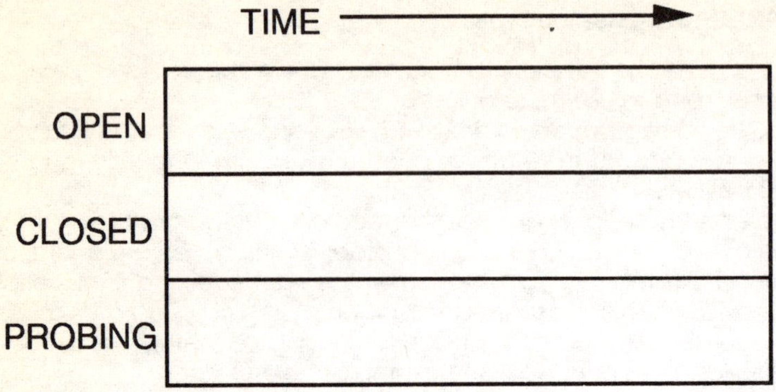

Figure 7.4   *Question types chart*

Leading questions

Leading questions are best avoided in most business situations, but
particularly when using counselling techniques. They steer the other
person to answer in a particular way.

There are two ways of asking leading questions. One is by tagging a
leading phrase such as 'isn't it', 'don't you', 'haven't we' onto the
beginning or end of your statement; for example, 'This is a wonderful
book, isn't it!', 'Don't you think this is a wonderful book?' The other is
by stating your own or someone else's opinion first, and then asking
the other for theirs: 'I think this is a wonderful book. What do you
think?'

Subordinates may answer leading questions unaware that they are
being led in their response, or they may be aware and feel annoyed
about being led.

To summarise the risks inherent in asking questions when
counselling:

- Too many questions will feel like an interrogation.
- Questioning might put control of the conversation with the
  manager, and not with the subordinate.
- The subordinate might then get too used to this conversational
  style and stop talking spontaneously, instead waiting for questions
  from the manager.

8

Challenging and confrontation

ounselling is not only about listening, accepting and showing empathy. It also means helping people to recognise and change their dysfunctional patterns of thinking and behaviour. The objective of challenging or confronting is to expand the subordinate's awareness in some area. We want to help them:

- to consider other ways of *interpreting* things, or
- to discover different ways of *dealing* with things.

An example of a distorted perception which can be challenged is over- or underrating oneself, and an example of unproductive coping behaviour which can be challenged is isolating oneself from colleagues. In the second example, the subordinate's perception of the situation (racist attitudes and comments, for example) may be accurate, but isolation from colleagues is not the most productive way of coping with these circumstances.

Challenging is the most difficult part of counselling for many people. It involves risk because the subordinate may react negatively to the challenge. Negative reactions to challenging are often due to oversensitivity to criticism, pride, or difficulty in admitting fault – especially if the view or behaviour pattern has been held for a long time, or you are dealing with a martyr-type personality who enjoys complaining more than changing. Also, they are likely to feel more comfortable with you in your empathetic mode than in your challenging mode, so they may try to change you (back to being empathetic only). Although challenging is difficult, if it is successful, it speeds the progress towards developing action plans.

WHEN TO CHALLENGE

Timing is very important. The challenge should occur *after* the first phase of developing the relationship has been established and the problem has been defined as the other person sees it. Your subordinate needs to have 'unloaded', quelled their emotions, and begun to feel 'safe'. Your challenge is much more likely to be listened to and considered once you have listened to and shown empathy with the subordinate, and they feel accepted and understood. You need to have gained a full understanding of the situation before challenging. An indicator that the subordinate is ready for challenging is when they start to challenge themselves – when they begin to show signs of questioning their own point of view or start constructively to analyse, evaluate and criticise themselves. In the example below the subordinate suddenly queries whether their own behaviour is contributing to the situation.

> *Subordinate:* 'I just don't understand! How could he continue behaving this way? Why won't he be honest and discuss things rationally? I can't trust anything he says any more. Maybe it's something I'm doing. Although I can't think what!'

There are exceptions to the above rule about waiting for the appropriate time to challenge, especially when using counselling skills in the workplace. In certain instances challenging will need to happen earlier in the process, for example:

- when the subordinate's behaviours are causing great distress to others;
- when the subordinate is very hostile towards you;
- when the subordinate's behaviour is affecting the unit's productivity quite adversely;
- when the subordinate's behaviours are very self-defeating;
- when there is time pressure to improve the situation.

These needs for early challenging should be explained to the subordinate.

There are times when it is inappropriate to challenge, for example when you are simply impatient or just in the mood for a fight, or when your subordinate is very emotional for any reason.

WHAT TO CHALLENGE

The following is a list of circumstances in which challenging may facilitate progress:

1. **Discrepancies between verbal, vocal and body messages**
   As discussed earlier, challenging is appropriate when different manners of communication indicate different things. Challenge to bring up the 'real' material which the person may feel hesitant about discussing.
   — *Example:*   Michael says everything is going well, but his fists are clenched, his body tense, and his words short and sharp.

2. **Incongruities between words and actions**   The person's actions may not conform with what they say.
   — *Example:*   Joan says she is interested in and committed to the ABC project, but she does not turn up at the project planning meetings.

3. **Incongruities between past and present remarks**   When attitudes expressed previously contradict attitudes expressed in the present.
   — *Example:*   Simon says he finds his project group difficult to get along with, whereas before he emphasised how productive the group was. He may have changed his mind, he may be ambivalent, or one or the other of the statements could have been hiding his real attitude. Challenge to find out what's going on.

4. **Unrealistic self-image**   Under- or over-rating themselves, or unaware of how they appear to others. When your own and others' experience of the subordinate are significantly different from their image of themselves. Challenge to point out that their perception of themselves does not match up with your own or that of others.

5. **Waffling, rambling**   Going off on tangents, talking in circles, overelaborating on trivial details, not talking about the real issues, not making sense. An indicator that they are waffling is your getting confused or bored. If you are bored, chances are that they are not talking incisively enough.

CASE EXAMPLE 3

A senior manager from a national health organisation wanted to improve his management skills. When I asked what in particular he wanted to work on, he proceeded to describe how wonderful his job was, how important he was in his company, and how nice his office was. He told me about the politics within his organisation, his achievements, and his reading in the field of psychology. He name-dropped many famous psychologists and business management gurus. He talked very loudly and quickly for about 10 minutes, and did not make much sense. At the end of all this I was a bit dumbfounded.

I repeated my question, 'So, what aspects of your management skills do you feel you need to work on?' He then began to explain that he was well liked as a manager, and had been cheered for wildly by his employees during a skit he performed at a company party. I asked him, 'Which parts of your job do you find most difficult?' He gave me an explanation of how to use fishbone diagrams and mind maps when running a meeting. I asked again, 'What did you come here to work on?' He looked down and said quietly, 'I suppose I tend to be too dominant.'

This is a simple (and somewhat amusing) example in that this person went from being indirect and protective to being direct, concise and honest, just by my having repeatedly asked the question in different ways. Often it takes more time and effort, especially when the person has well-developed defence mechanisms. And people can be quite skilled in their efforts to confuse or mislead you regarding the real problem, even when a part of them really wants to open up.

6. **Misinformation/misperceptions**   Inaccurate information or things missing from the picture. Generalisations and exaggerations. Encourage them to consider information which will give them a more objective view of the situation. Or they may need to be reminded about points forgotten or overlooked. Their point of view may be keeping them locked into their problem situation and possibly even creating their problems.

7. **Overlooked alternatives**   When the person is not acknowledging that there are alternative courses of action other than the one they have chosen. Encourage them to talk about what *they* can do in the future rather than about what others are doing to them. People often need to realise that their own action or inaction are contributing to a situation which they are entirely blaming on others. If they say there is nothing they can do to improve the situation, urge them to analyse whether this is indeed the case or whether they simply *won't* do something different. If they could be doing something different, they need to look into why they aren't or why they don't want to.

8. **Over-focused on past or future**   to the detriment of the present.

9. **Self-destructive beliefs**
   — *'Should', 'ought' or 'must' beliefs*   These are beliefs that we were taught as children by our parents, our religion, or by society. Sometimes they are traditional beliefs which have been passed down without much thought given to them. Often people feel guilty if they do not go along with these 'rules'. Or, if they do go along with them, they feel annoyed about being compelled to 'follow the rules' when they do not want to. They may not realise that they have a choice in

the matter. For example, consider the rule 'One must not be rude.' There is a time and place for saying what you think even if it might be considered rude, but someone who rigidly follows this belief may be unable to, which could cause them great difficulty. To help people whose 'shoulds', 'oughts', and 'musts' are getting in their way, challenge to awaken their awareness of what is happening, to explore what the beliefs are (often these are sub-conscious beliefs), where they come from, and the effects they are having

— *Irrational beliefs* People sometimes have unrealistic or unfair beliefs which, although they may not be operating at a conscious level, can be making life very difficult for them and those they work with. The following chart lists some common irrational beliefs and some alternative rational beliefs which we can help them to adopt instead.

Irrational Belief	*Rational Alternative*
I must never make mistakes.	The only way not to make mistakes is to do nothing. I'm active, and all active people make mistakes.
Other people should not make mistakes.	No one is perfect. I can accept that other people will make mistakes.
Other people make me angry.	I make myself angry when I don't accept that other people don't live up to my expectations.
Other people should live up to my expectations.	Other people don't need to live up to my expectations.
My happiness depends on other people's behaviour and attitudes	My happiness comes from within me and does not depend on others.
I must live up to other people's expectations.	I don't need to live up to other people's expectations to be OK.
I must win.	According to the law of averages most people only win 50 per cent of the time. I don't need to win to feel OK.
Life should be fair and just.	Life is not fair and just.

I must get my own way	I do not need to get my own way to feel OK, and can sometimes get satisfaction out of letting other people have their own way.
I need other people's approval to feel OK.	It is nice to get others' approval, but I do not need their approval to feel OK.
I must always please other people.	It is unrealistic to expect that I can always please other people.
I must never get angry.	It is OK to be angry sometimes.
I must not cry.	It is OK to cry.
I can't be happy if people misjudge me.	People sometimes misjudge me. That is inevitable. But I know that I am OK and that is what matters.

Source: © Geldard, 1993, from *Basic Personal Counselling*, Prentice Hall, Australia.

10. **Self-destructive behaviour** When subordinates are not recognising or considering the consequences of their behaviours. Encourage them to explore their behaviours in order to understand them better and to change them. Look into the motivations and meanings behind behaviours.
    — *Example:* Bill is competent in his work, but irritates others, both senior and junior to him, with his excessive and sometimes flippant use of humour.

11. **Stuck in a mode** General passiveness, martyr mode, over-optimistic, overpessimistic, victim mode, blaming. The person may be contributing to a problem which *they* are attributing to external forces.
    — *Example:* Susan is overworked. She blames others for giving her too much to do and for taking advantage of her helpful nature. She resents being 'the responsible one' and sees the others as irresponsible. But at the same time she seems to take pride in being so important and needed.

12. **Refusal to see other points of view.**

13. **Reluctance to act on intentions.**

14. **Topics/facts avoided** Relevant things which the person does *not* talk about. They are avoiding a basic issue which seems to be bothering them.

15. **Feeling abnormal** Thinking their feelings are not normal. Distress can often be greatly reduced if the person can begin to understand that their feelings are normal given the situation.

People worry that they are crazy because they have certain feelings, and they often feel very guilty about negative feelings, for example feeling angry with someone for dying. The charts of stages (life stages, transition stages) in Part IV are useful for understanding emotional reactions. It is very important for managers to have an understanding of these emotional responses, as well as the behavioural responses which result from them, in order to help subordinates understand what is happening to them.

16. **Repeated themes in conversation/recognised patterns in behaviour** By listening to the person talk and considering how different parts of their dialogue have similarities or could somehow be related, you can give feedback on recurring themes or patterns which they may be unaware of.

WAYS TO CHALLENGE

There are two methods of challenging: pushing and pulling. These are the fundamental categories of influencing. Pushing is being directive: telling, demanding, explaining your reasoning. Pulling is facilitative challenging through questioning. Pulling is slower and gentler, but usually more effective, gaining greater commitment to change on the other person's part. In most cases it is best to attempt challenging by pulling first, and resort to pushing only when pulling is not working quickly enough.

Pushing may inhibit rather than open up the individual. They can become defensive, angry, withdrawn, rebellious or upset. If they are submissive, then pushing can make them more dependent on your opinions, instead of more independent. However, there are a few people who can handle the pushing approach and prefer it to the pulling approach. These people have strong egos and prefer that you 'tell it to them straight'. You need to know the person you are working with to assess how well they can take and appreciate direct challenge. If they can handle it, the push approach is quicker. If you are going to push, do it clearly and concisely. If what you are saying is your own interpretation or someone else's opinion, then acknowledge that. It is appropriate to push when you are simply correcting misinformation.

Because the pulling approach encourages self challenging and criticism, it engenders more self-responsibility, self-confidence and commitment to change. Pulling takes the form of asking questions and making suggestions tentatively and carefully, usually in the form of questions.

In the example below, Manager 1 makes a pushing challenge, whereas Manager 2 makes a pulling challenge.

Manager 1: 'Other people don't see it that way. They think that you are being obstinate and difficult. People are reluctant to approach you now.'

Manager 2: 'How do you think the others view your behaviour?'

Instead of telling a subordinate what others' points of views could be, you can first try asking them to imagine how another person might be feeling. In this situation, if after attempting the pulling approach the subordinate cannot conceive how others are thinking, then the manager can always use the pushing method.

If you choose the pushing method be careful how you word it. Manager 1 below is too harsh. Manager 2 pushes in a more respectful manner, and Manager 3 pulls.

Manager 1: 'It's your own fault you know. You ignore or dismiss everything he says during the discussions we have. No wonder he won't cooperate with you on the project.'

Manager 2: 'I think he might be behaving uncooperatively because he feels ignored by you. He seems to be disappointed when he is not responded to. What do you think?'

Manager 3: 'Why do you think he doesn't want to cooperate? Could there be a reason he feels uncooperative towards you?'

CASE EXAMPLE 4

George worked in a computer firm and had been offered an opportunity to move from his present position as a programmer to work at a more senior level as a trainer. He was apprehensive about the new job, never having worked with people much before. He was concerned that he was meant to be a 'techie' and that he didn't have the right personality for training. As I talked to him, he came across to me as a thoughtful, warm person, with an ability to listen and a lively sense of humour. I predicted that given some counselling, training and coaching, he could be a very competent trainer. But there was also the possibility that George simply had no interest in training. I did not share any of my thoughts initially. Instead I took him through a line of questioning in order to understand him, and to challenge his thinking.

George: 'I am not the man for the job.'

Me: 'What would the right man be like?'

George: 'Articulate, confident, and good at understanding people.'

Me:	'How articulate do you think you are?'
George:	'Well, I can explain things well enough to individuals when they come to ask me questions, but I don't know how to manage a whole group of people all at the same time.'
Me:	'Is managing a group of people an inborn or a learned skill?'
George:	'I suppose people do learn it, but probably some are naturally better at it than others. I don't think I will be good at it.'
Me:	'And if you don't think that you have this "natural" ability, what makes you think that?'
George:	'I am much better at working by myself with things than with people.'
Me:	'Why do you have the idea that you don't work as well with people?'
George:	'I don't know. I just don't feel right. I don't feel I belong in a training position.'
Me:	'What could be the reasons for your feeling you don't belong in a training position?'
George:	(getting impatient) 'I don't know. It's just how I think based on what I know of myself!'
Me:	'Well, for example, could your feelings be natural nervousness regarding doing something new, or have you encountered bad experiences managing groups of people, or do you not like the idea of training, or has someone in your past told you that you are better with machines than people, or can you think of any other possible reasons?'
George:	'No, it is just how I understand myself.'
Me:	'Why do you think you were chosen for this position?'
George:	(silence) 'Well, I suppose people do tend to come to me with questions. I am just uncomfortable about the idea of being a trainer. Maybe it is just apprehension, but I don't know.'
Me:	'Do you think you would enjoy training if you learned the skills needed?'

etc...

There are, of course, many ways to challenge given the same situation. The following are some examples:

Misinformation/misperception

Sometimes people tend to see things in a pessimistic way. We can't dismiss their negative feelings because there is probably a valid reason for them seeing things negatively. So simply telling them not to be pessimistic won't help. But through skilful challenging with questions, you can sometimes help them to change the way they perceive events and situations. You can help them to have a more objective way of seeing things by questioning them about positive aspects of the situation. Or you can ask them if they can come up with more constructive ways of dealing with the situation.

Subordinate:	'My newest member of staff, John, is continuously in and out of my office. He is asking me to help him with things he could easily resolve for himself. He knows how busy I am. Quite frankly, John has become a bit of a pest, taking up my time. It has got to the point now where I am quite irritable when I speak to him.'
Manager:	(pulling) 'I can understand that this must be a nuisance when you are so busy. What do you think is going on in John's mind?'

If the subordinate does not think of any positive ideas, the manager can then suggest the positive side in the form of a question.

Manager:	'It seems that your input is very important to John. Do you think he may be wanting to get to know you a bit better or to communicate with you a bit more?'

The manager has offered another interpretation of John's behaviour. Instead of seeing it as a negative nuisance, it can be regarded in a positive way, in that John, being a fairly recent addition to the staff, may be trying to build up a relationship with his boss, at a time when the boss is very busy. Maybe John simply feels unnoticed. The manager's interpretation could be wrong, however, which is why it is important to put forward interpretations tentatively. It could be that John is anxious and doesn't want to make any mistakes.

Discrepancies between verbal, vocal and body messages

Manager:	'You say you are fine, but I see you looking tired and sounding down. Your voice seems lower and quieter than normal.'

Incongruity between words and actions

Manager:	'You have said that you are not overworked in your new position, but I am a bit confused because I've noticed that you frequently look rushed or harried, and that you are staying in

the office much longer than usual in the evenings.'

Unrealistic self-image

Manager: 'You describe yourself as really struggling with managing project teams, yet I see you as being quite competent in this area and I think my colleagues see you as being competent as well. Why do you think there is this discrepancy in our views?' or 'Do you think you may be expecting too much of yourself?'

Waffling, rambling

You need to take action to focus the conversation. This can be done by pointing out what you have noticed is happening and asking the person to focus the conversation on the items of significance. Ask them for what is important and get them to focus.

Manager: 'It seems that the conversation is digressing from what is most important to you, and I am aware that we only have 35 minutes left.'

When the subordinate talks in a general sense and is not specific enough for you to understand the crux of the problem, you can ask for more precise information.

Subordinate: 'I can never get through to Michael.'
Manager: 'In what specific ways do you find it difficult to get through to him?'
Subordinate: 'Michael never listens to me. He ignores me in meetings. In fact, he won't even look at me. And he walks away when I am speaking to him.'

Other phrases you could use to encourage specifics:

■ 'Explain to me what you mean by ...'
■ 'Can you give me an example of ...'

Overlooked alternatives

Manager: 'Do you see any similarities between the predicament that you are in and situations that others have been in? What might others have done to improve such a situation?'

CASE EXAMPLE 5

John was having difficulty with his marriage. He had been moody and irritable at work for quite a while and his colleagues were losing patience with him. He seemed to expect that everyone else would just put up with him until things improved at home and then he would be in better spirits. His boss, William, expressed concern that if John's attitude continued his future within the organisation might be affected. He suggested that they meet to talk about things.

William started out the meeting by expressing his desire to help John. John explained that he did not think there was much that could be done. His wife had stopped taking temporary calming prescription drugs and was on a waiting list to see a therapist. Meanwhile, John said, he was suffering her very quick temper and unpredictable crying spells. He said that until his wife sorted herself out there was nothing he could do. He spoke angrily at length describing details of his wife's constant raging and tantrums, but he did not discuss his own feelings or plans.

When William asked him about himself he said he was miserable and would leave his wife if he could, but that he was unable to because of his four-year-old son. When William attempted to pull more out of him John would only say, 'I have no choices. I could not hurt my son.'

John claimed that the situation was completely the fault of his wife, and that he had no options. There were three related areas in John's thinking which William wanted to challenge: that the son should be a reason for John not even to consider his options, that there were no steps of action he could take, and that the problems in the marriage were all due to his wife.

William decided that in order to get John to consider all of his options, he first had to challenge his thinking regarding his son. He chose to challenge this by 'pushing', because if John believed that parents splitting up is the worst choice possible for a child, then it would be difficult to challenge him by pulling. So William explained to John a bit of child psychology regarding quality parenting. Once John was convinced that in some situations staying together is not in the child's best interest, then he was able to acknowledge at least one other option – leaving.

At this point William had a choice between 'pushing' again and explaining to John about how relationships deteriorate because of the actions (or inaction) of *both* partners, or 'pulling' by questioning him regarding his own responsibilities within the relationship. He chose to try pulling first using questions such as:

- What complaints or concerns does your wife have about you?
- Is there a possibility that your own behaviours could be contributing to the tension?
- How do you know whether you are presently acting in the best possible way?
- If you plan to try to stay in the relationship, are there actions that you could take to try to improve things?
- If you found a way to take action yourself, could that then help you to function better at work?

John got a little hostile, explaining that his wife complained continuously about everything and exploded regularly over little things,
and that he reacted by commenting on the quantity of her complaints and the excessiveness of her anger. William asked whether he
had ever read any books on communicating within relationships, and
whether he had sought advice himself from any professionals. By
asking questions which helped John to see that he did not have
enough knowledge to know how best to handle situations with his
wife, William was able to help John to consider that there were other
actions he could take besides leaving his wife or staying in the relationship and expecting her to make all the changes.

Self-destructive beliefs

Supervisor: 'I just can't figure out a fairer way to divide up
the sales territories. No matter what I do
someone will be unhappy and I will be seen as
unfair.'

Manager: 'You seem to think that you must make life 100
per cent fair for your sales team. Do you think
that this is possible?'

Stuck in a mode

Here is an example of being stuck in panic mode:

Subordinate: 'I am terrified of speaking to everyone at the
next board meeting. I am flattered to have been
asked to present the plan for the XYZ Project
I've been working on, but the thought of getting
up in front of all those people who can affect
my future is giving me grey hairs.'

Manager: (*after* reflecting feelings and getting subordinate to discuss them thoroughly) 'So you
are very apprehensive about the board presentation, especially since it feels very important to your career. Could you possibly think of
your nervous anxiety as nervous excitement –
excitement about an opportunity to shine and
impress everyone?'

Reluctance to act on intentions

Manager: 'You keep mentioning that you would like to
develop yourself further and to extend beyond

your research position into consultancy. Have you taken actions to start moving yourself towards the consultant's position?'

Repeated themes in conversation/recognised patterns in behaviour

Manager: 'You have talked about three areas which are troubling you: not having enough contact with your subordinates to keep on top of things, being unable to monitor the accuracy of the packaging and shipping department when they send out your products, and being unable to get your teenagers to listen to you at home. All three of these problems involve control. It seems as if lack of control is an issue for you at the moment.'

TIPS FOR FACILITATIVE CHALLENGING

It is not a good idea to suddenly change from being empathetic to being completely confrontational. Challenging needs to be approached slowly and little by little. Mix in empathetic responses with your challenges and they are likely to be much better received. A useful approach is to reflect what the subordinate has said and immediately follow with a challenge. The reflection reminds them that they have been heard and understood, before offering a different perception.

If you give advice, making statements like 'If I were you . . .', then you are not counselling. That is talking down to the other person.

When you need to give feedback, either your own opinion or others', then do not treat those opinions as being statements of fact. Using 'I' statements rather than 'you' statements helps to achieve this ownership. For example, the statement 'I found your report difficult to follow because the order of the topics did not make sense to me' will be better received than a statement like 'Your writing does not make sense because you didn't put the topics in a logical order.' Even worse would be a statement like 'You are not a logical writer', which makes a judgement about the person rather than commenting on the behaviour. This sort of statement is very likely to get a negative reaction.

A statement of your feelings is useful too. The statement 'I am a bit confused' (in the example above for challenging incongruity between words and actions) softens the challenge because it raises a query rather than stating an argument.

Sometimes a simple summary of what the other person has said will make them hear if they are being unfair, one-sided or biased. They may then bring up the other's point of view or another way of looking at things.

Manager:	'Are you saying that your department needs exclusive access to the Mac equipment?'
Subordinate:	'Well, I suppose the other departments need to use it sometimes. It's just that we use it more than any other, and we usually need it on short notice. Perhaps it would be better if we bought new machines especially for our department.'

When adopting a counselling style, you must allow opportunity for you to be confronted by the subordinate as well. This occasion can be used by you to set an example of how to think about and respond to challenges and confrontations.

Talk about your own and others' experiences only as a last resort, and then tentatively – acknowledging that the situations are not necessarily exactly the same.

It is very important to put challenges over extremely tentatively when you are unsure of whether the challenge is correct or not. You do not want to hold back from challenging for fear of upsetting the subordinate, but if you learn to put forward your ventured challenges carefully, you can then raise issues and considerations whilst minimising the risk of offending.

Do not overdo the challenging because you might discourage the subordinate. Unless the case is severe, leave the ultimate problem 'diagnosis' and decision-making responsibility up to them.

EXERCISE 15   Challenging

Think of the last times you were in situations where someone presented you with the circumstances below. What could you have said to challenge the person in the most constructive way? Assume for the sake of this exercise that rapport and empathy have already been established. Write out your challenges in the spaces below the statements.

Waffling, rambling

_____

_____

_____

_____

_____

Misinformation/misperceptions

_____

_____

_____

_____

_____

Incongruities between words and actions

_____

_____

_____

_____

_____

Incongruities between past and present remarks

_____

_____

_____

_____

_____

Irrational beliefs

_____

_____

_____

_____

_____

Unrealistic self-image

_____

_____

_____

_____

_____

Discrepancies between verbal, vocal and body messages

_____

_____

_____

_____

_____

Overlooked alternatives

_____

_____

_____

_____

_____

9

Problem solving/problem management

Having gained new perceptions and insights into his or her problems, what can your subordinate now do or stop doing to improve the situation? There are many books on the process of problem solving. You may prefer to work through a specific model of your own. This chapter will cover the general concepts which you need to be aware of in order to help people with problem management.

The steps in problem solving/management include:

- General goal.
- Specific objectives.
- Objective prioritisation.
- Strategy for action.
- Monitoring of implementation.

GENERAL GOAL

In order to increase the chances of your subordinates putting the necessary time and effort into executing the problem-solving steps, it is important that they take full responsibility for managing the problem, and commit themselves to their goal. You need to make sure they are convinced that the goal is both beneficial and achievable, and are willing to put in enough effort in working towards it. The goals and the action steps have to feel to them as if they are their own, and not yours or someone else's.

In order to help your subordinates to determine their goal, it is useful to ask them: 'What alternatives exist?', 'How could things be different?', or 'What would you like to be able to do differently?'

Negative definitions of problems can be turned into positive goals. For example: 'Stop overreacting and being irritable with staff' can be translated into 'Managing difficult staff situations more calmly and rationally'.

The subordinate's goal is likely to be a very general one, such as 'To become more effective in meetings' or 'To be a better supervisor'. The next step is to break the goal down into objectives which are specific enough to work with.

SPECIFIC OBJECTIVES

Objectives need to be clear and specific enough to apply action plans to. In order to help the subordinate to turn a goal into more precise objectives, you can ask questions such as (Egan, 1990):

- 'What would the current problem "look like" if it were better?'
- 'What would you be doing that you are not doing now?'
- 'What would you stop doing that you are doing now?'

Are new behaviours going to be added, or old behaviours decreased in frequency, or is a new behaviour going to replace an old behaviour? For example, a supervisor's objectives might be fewer losses of temper, scripting feedback before meeting with staff, and making an effort to improve his or her communication with the department's secretaries.

Objectives have to be realistic and achievable, otherwise subordinates will become discouraged. Sometimes they will be dealing with changing very long-term habits. It is a good idea for the objectives to be time-bound realistically in order both to motivate and avoid eternal procrastination. In other words, the objectives should include an approximate time horizon stating when the objective will be achieved by – eg in the next month, in the next quarter?

OBJECTIVE PRIORITISATION

Next, the objectives need to be prioritised. Your subordinates will not be able to do everything at once, and they will become demotivated if they try to do so.

They could prioritise in order of importance. Or you could suggest that they prioritise the objectives based on those which, when addressed, will affect more than one area of their work (those which will have the most far-reaching effects). The subordinates do not necessarily need to start with the most severe problem – that might have to be worked up to. The limitations of their schedule might also make one order of priorities more practical than another.

STRATEGY FOR ACTION

Subordinates now need to formulate action plans which will enable them to achieve their objectives. Work with the objectives, one at a time, in order of priority. You can help them to think about how to achieve the objective – to consider and choose among the different strategy options available.

It is very important that they do consider a range of alternative action plans for achieving the goal, and that the implications of these are contemplated carefully before action is taken. This means helping them to avoid the temptation to jump in and run with the first idea that comes to mind. Their plan needs to fit in with their overall lifestyle, goals and values. It should make sense, be practical, and have realistic timing.

The following types of questions will help to stimulate subordinates' imaginations to come up with creative ways of achieving their goals (Egan, 1990):

1. **How?**   How can you get where you would like to go? How many different ways are there to accomplish what you want to accomplish?
2. **Who?**   Who can help you to achieve your goal? What people can serve as resources for the accomplishment of this goal?
3. **What?**   What resources both inside yourself and outside are needed for you to accomplish your goals?
4. **Where?**   What places can help you achieve your goal?
5. **When?**   What times or what kind of timing would be best for you to achieve your goal? Is one time better than another?

Once you have tried to get subordinates to come up with their ideas, then you may want to put forward some suggestions of your own. The way that these suggestions are put forward is very important. If the suggestions are made as statements, there are risks that the subordinate might either agree out of compliance at the time, but then not go ahead and follow the suggestion; or that they might rebel against the solution put forward because it is not their own idea, even though they might have readily accepted it given time to think about it properly.

A better approach for making suggestions is to put them in the form of questions – 'What do you think about doing X?', 'How do you feel about Y idea?', 'Could you do X?', 'What would happen if ...', 'What are the pros and cons of doing A?' This last question is helpful because it asks the other person to consider both positives and negatives, and therefore seems more neutral.

Along with action plans, ways of monitoring progress should be planned at this stage. Methods of monitoring are discussed in the following section.

MONITORING OF IMPLEMENTATION

The subordinate has to decide how they will monitor their efforts and progress. If their action plans fail, they need to focus on what can be learned from the experience. And, if circumstances have changed, they should be encouraged not to give up, but to adjust the action plan accordingly.

The provision of motivators and support is vital in order to inspire action. Subordinates can keep themselves motivated by self-recognition for progress achieved. They need to give themselves regular incentives. Small rewards earned after little steps have been taken generally work better than one large reward obtained once the overall goal has been achieved. Rewarding themselves for taking action is necessary, irrespective of whether the desired results ensue!

The rewards which subordinates give themselves should be small things which they enjoy, but which they would not normally do for themselves. If the rewards are too expensive, subordinates won't be able to reward themselves frequently enough, and if the rewards are things they are getting now, then they will not be novel enough. Bouquets of flowers, luxury food items and magazines make good rewards.

Support is invaluable for someone who is trying to make changes. You can suggest that the subordinate find sources of support to call upon, for example: a colleague, the company training or personnel department, their partner, a friend or a support group.

Once the skills of problem management (from identifying the problem to setting goals to taking action) have been learned, the subordinate can then implement this process more independently in other areas of their work.

Example of Problem Solving:

1. General goal.
    —   After expressing feelings about the situations with his boss, his colleagues and his partner, the subordinate defines his problem generally as relationship difficulties. His goal is to improve his relationships.

2. Breaking down the problem into its components.
    —   Having been probed to think about what causes relationship
        difficulties, the subordinate comes up with the following:
        (a) Impatience and harried irritability.
        (b) Bitterness from those he was promoted over.
        (c) Lack of listening to others.
        (d) Procrastination in dealing with things.
        (e) Not enough time in the day.
3. Determining specific objectives.
    —   Manager asks subordinate what he would like do differently
        in order to improve his relationships. Subordinate comes
        up with:
        (a) Be more calm and controlled.
        (b) Become a better listener.
        (c) Improve time management.
4. Prioritising objectives.
    —   Manager asks subordinate to consider which of these three
        takes priority. Subordinate prioritises goals in the following
        order:
        (a) Become a better listener.
        (b) Be more calm and controlled.
        (c) Improve time management.
5. Determining concrete steps to achieve goal 1.
    —   Manager asks subordinate to think about what steps need to
        be taken in order to become a better listener. Subordinate
        says:
        (a) Read some books about listening.
        (b) Try to listen more during conversations.
    —   Manager wants to make some of the steps more concrete.
        'Try to listen more during conversations' is a bit vague. How
        would we know when this had been achieved? Manager
        asks subordinate, 'When exactly, where, how and with
        whom do you plan to do this? How will you monitor your-
        self?' Subordinate then rewrites steps as:
        (a) Ask communications consultant for a recommended
             reading list on listening.
        (b) Pick two books from the list and read them while
             travelling to visit clients.
        (c) Listen more than speak during the first half of my
             regular Monday morning meeting with my boss.
        (d) After each meeting make a note of how well I am able
             to achieve this.
        (e) After four meetings ask boss whether she has noticed a
             difference.

6. Take first action step(s).
   — Subordinate goes off. Puts plan into action.
7. Review progress and reward self for taking action.
   — At a later date manager asks about progress. Subordinate reports that although he has a long way to go to becoming a 'good' listener, he has begun to make some progress. The books he has read have given him some very useful tips. He has kept records on his meetings with his boss, and knows that he has been listening for a higher percentage of the time than he used to. Unfortunately, his boss had not noticed the difference. Manager reminds subordinate that regardless of others' appreciation or lack of it, he must reward himself for his achievements in whatever small but meaningful way he can. Subordinate buys chocolates on the way home from work on days he has made significant efforts.
8. Review overall plan.
   — Subordinate decides plan is working well so far. He will find two more areas in his life where he can systematically apply and monitor his listening skills. Manager asks subordinate how he might apply a similar problem-solving process in order to achieve the objective of 'being more calm and controlled'.

10

Decision making

Decisions are difficult because they are usually not black and white. Pros and cons must be weighed, which makes decision making frustrating, confusing and possibly even frightening, rather than cut and dried. When there are losses no matter which option is chosen, your subordinate may resist making a decision. However, once they become aware of this and come to accept that there will be an inevitable loss no matter what, it will become easier to make the decision. If you work through decision making with them using one of the processes below in a counselling style, then they will have a tool which will make them more self-reliant in decision making in the future.

When working with a subordinate on decision making, if possible do not push too quickly for a decision then and there. Leave them to their own devices. Sometimes people just need time to think.

FORCEFIELD ANALYSIS

One useful device to introduce to subordinates struggling with decision making is forcefield analysis. This is helpful for making a simple decision such as whether or not to take an action. The process considers and weighs the forces operating for and against the particular action.

For example, Chris is trying to decide whether to buy a new brand of software package for the department, or to stick with the one they are already using. Taking the decision to buy the software, the forces for and against are listed on opposite sides.

Buying New Software

Forces For	*Forces Against*
Faster speed of processing	Expense of purchase
Extra customised data fields	Time and cost of retraining staff
Easier to make enquiries into system	Will need to change entry forms which other departments use
0800 software support service	

Then the forces are ranked for importance (1–10, 1–5, . . .) and totals for each side are calculated.

Buying New Software (1 to 10)

Forces For +16		*Forces Against* −18	
Faster speed of processing	3	Expense of purchase	7
Extra customised data fields	6	Time and cost of retraining staff	9
Easier to make enquiries into system	5	Will need to change entry forms which other departments use	2
0800 software support service	2		

It is important to recognise that a decision should not be made based on the resulting numbers. A higher total for forces acting against buying the new software package in the above example does not necessarily make not buying it the appropriate decision. The subordinate needs to reconsider the weightings and check for any omitted forces. Forcefield analysis is a tool to assist thinking about decisions in a systematic manner – for displaying the pros and cons in a manner which is easy to review. It does not necessarily provide the definitive answer.

The subordinate should remember to consider pros and cons both to the company and its goals and to other people/departments as well as to themselves.

Decision making becomes more complex when there are several alternatives to be considered. Possible questions to consider when comparing alternatives include (Pokras, 1989):

■ Which option seems most workable?
■ Which solution has the best chance of success?
■ How expensive is each possible solution?

- How much time will each solution involve?
- How risky is each possible solution?
- Which solution can everyone decide to commit to fully?

Pokras also suggests useful processes for comparing alternatives, such as the consequences worksheet and the criteria matrix.

CONSEQUENCES WORKSHEET

A consequences worksheet helps subordinates to compare whether the possible benefits and rewards of certain actions or solutions

Solution	Potential costs	Potential risks	Possible benefits	Possible rewards	Conclusions

Figure 10.1 *Consequences worksheet*

Source: Pokras, 1989.

justify the potential costs and risks. Possible benefits and rewards are considered relative to subordinates' personal performance plans and departmental and organisational objectives. Potential costs and risks are considered by predicting ramifications.

CRITERIA MATRIX

A criteria matrix is an organised and quantifiable method for visualising alternatives. Alternative solutions are listed vertically in the left-hand column and the criteria to measure them are listed horizontally across the top. Ratings go inside the grid, and total ratings for the solutions go in the last column (on the right).

Alternative Solutions	Evaluation Criteria					Total Rating

Figure 10.2 *Criteria matrix*

Source: Adapted from Pokras, 1989.

Ratings can vary in their complexity. You could use a +, – or ? scale; an A,B,C label; or a numerical scale (1 to 3, 1 to 10, ...).

Alternative Solutions	Evaluation Criteria					Total Rating
	Accuracy	Cost	Morale	Confident-iality		
Hire Full-Time Staff	5	1	4	5		15
Hire Part-Time Staff	5	3	4	4		16
Hire Temporary Staff	2	4	2	1		9

Figure 10.3 *Sample criteria matrix*

Once again, the ratings will need to be reconsidered for congruity once the grid is completed. The grid's result is only as accurate as the individual scores.

11

Other elements of counselling

OPENING

At the beginning of a counselling session, it is essential to establish an appropriate atmosphere. An invitation to the subordinate to talk is conveyed by your posture, manner, gestures, tone of voice and words.

Equality in the relationship also needs to be confirmed. As a manager there will be many times when you *do* take the position of authority and lead, and your subordinate may expect that from you. So it is all the more important to establish that *this* discussion is going to operate in a counselling style and therefore will be a meeting of equals. Do this early on by setting up the room appropriately, displaying listening responses, and by encouraging your subordinate to take responsibility to help themselves.

When your subordinate enters the room, greet them warmly using their name, and offer them a seat. Then say something which makes them feel welcome and acknowledged, and communicates that it is up to them to define the problem as they see it, and that you are ready to listen.

The following are examples of appropriate openers:

- 'Good morning, Jill. Please have a seat. How can I help you?'
- '... What is on your mind?'
- '... I understand you want to talk about ...'
- '... Tell me about the situation.'

If you, not they, have initiated the conversation, then:

- 'You don't seem yourself. Is anything going on? I've got some time if you'd like to talk.'

Not seeming rushed is important, but clear time boundaries should be set at the start, along with limitations on confidentiality (if appropriate). If the meeting is only going to be partially conducted in a counselling style, then it is a good idea to let the subordinate know which parts this applies to and which parts will be otherwise.

Physical set-up

The room set-up and seating arrangement can greatly contribute to but also detract from the creation of the right environment. Both communicate your attitudes in a subtle but significant way.

Chairs placed at a slight angle to one another generally make people much more comfortable than chairs placed straight across from one another. Figure 11.1 shows that by sitting directly opposite someone (Position A), it is easy to feel confrontational. Sitting at a 90 degree angle (Position B) is better, but not ideal because this angle can take away too much of the eye contact. Sitting at an angle slightly off head-on (Position C) is the ideal arrangement for counselling. This way it is easy to observe the other person and make direct eye contact, but also easy to break eye contact at times when it is uncomfortable.

It is best to use either no table or a low coffee table so that physical barriers will be limited and body language can be observed. If a table is necessary for papers and writing, then considerations should be made. Figure 11.2 illustrates that a small round table is more flexible than a square or rectangular table or desk because there is a range of angles at which you can place the chairs. If you must use a table with sides then sit at right angles on one corner rather than straight across, and turn the chairs slightly towards one another. Comfortable soft chairs are a nice touch, but if they are too low and soft they are not conducive to a serious atmosphere.

You should give some thought to the room chosen for the interview ahead of time. Rather than meeting in your office or your subordinate's, a neutral meeting room, such as a small conference room, will help to take away distractions and power differentials. Whatever room you end up using, try to prepare it ahead of time. It is best to have it as tidy and as empty as possible, at least with a clear desk. Put a

A   B   C

Figure 11.1

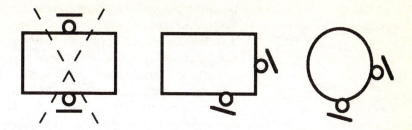

Figure 11.2

clock where you will be able to see it without looking at it obviously –
on a table next to your subordinate but facing you, for example, or on
a wall or shelf behind them. Remember to close the door to ensure
privacy and to plan for someone to take your calls to avoid interruptions. This gives the subordinate the impression that their issue is
important, and that they are the total focus of your attention.

CLOSING

You will need to prepare your subordinate for the end of the
counselling interview. About 10 minutes before time runs out, tell
them how much time is left. It is useful for them to be aware of the
limitation on the remaining time so that they can decide how they
want to use it. They may want to go into an area not covered yet, or to
go deeper into an area previously only touched on.

Then, two or three minutes from the end, summarise the main
points covered during the meeting. If you plan to meet again, arrange
the time and summarise action to be taken by either of you before
the next meeting. If you will not be meeting again, then leave the
subordinate with some positive feedback (for example, courage in
raising a difficult issue) or something constructive to think about.

| Area Manager to Retail Store Manager: | 'I see we're running out of time. Let's see if we can pull together what we've covered. You began by explaining why you are becoming dissatisfied in your current position as you approach retirement age. You feel more and more removed from your staff, both by age and style, and you would like to move to the IT depart- ment at central office, where you can make use of your favourite hobby and |

pastime, computing, during your last five years. You are aware that this has only been a whim up to now, but that you are feeling more and more discontented as time goes on. During the course of our conversation, you have determined that it is time to do something. Maybe between now and next time we meet you could do the networking you suggested, in order to see if your skills could be used in that department.'

You may find that you have to be quite firm about finishing. A good listener is hard to come by, and some people will want to hang on to you and keep you there as long as possible. If your subordinate does not conclude the interview themselves after your reminders about the time, then you must firmly end the conversation by saying something like 'I'm afraid we're going to have to stop now.'

REFERRAL

A manager who is proficient in counselling skills will tend to attract people to come to him or her with their problems, and will run into situations where it is not appropriate to help with the problem. Instead the subordinate needs to be referred elsewhere. How do you decide when to refer? *Always* refer when you feel you are out of your depth – when the problem is such that you do not feel qualified to help, you feel uncomfortable in doing so, or you do not have the resources. Also you should refer when time constraints do not allow you to help. Do not try to take on everything yourself. Be aware of when professional help is needed and what sorts of professional help are available (see Appendix A).

A manager should stick to dealing with 'here and now' problems, not deeply ingrained or long-term emotional problems which require a more permanent and professional nurturing relationship to heal. If you do not refer when you are out of your depth you could make matters worse. If you encounter a situation where phases 1 and 2 (developing the trust required for openness and defining the problem) are going to take a long time, then it is likely that the subordinate would be better off referred to a professional.

KEEPING THE FOCUS ON THE OTHER PERSON

When your subordinate focuses excessively on another person (or people), it is important to redirect the conversation towards their focusing on themselves, and taking responsibility for their own actions. Often people will talk about difficulties in the third person – 'He said . . ., she said . . ., he did . . ., she did . . .' Valuable time will be wasted if the focus is not kept on the subordinate and their own feelings and actions. Discussing others overextensively is not going to help the subordinate to decide what action to take for themselves.

Subordinate:	'My assistant has frequently been absent recently. He is going through a divorce, and I think he is finding it very stressful. I am finding it difficult to cope without him, especially since his absences are sporadic and unpredictable.'
Manager 1:	'So your assistant is going through a difficult divorce.'
Subordinate:	'My assistant has frequently been absent recently. He is going through a divorce, and I think he is finding it very stressful. I am finding it difficult to cope without him, especially since his absences are sporadic and unpredictable.'
Manager 2:	'You are frustrated at not knowing when he will be out of the office.'

Manager 2 was able to keep the focus on the subordinate, whereas Manager 1 was directing the conversation towards externals – the assistant, the difficult divorce.

Encourage your subordinate to focus on themselves by using 'I' statements rather than outwardly focused 'he', 'she' or 'they' statements. This will promote acknowledgement of their feelings, thoughts and actions, and ownership of their problems.

Focusing on externals is very common, especially since those who come to us often really believe that the problem belongs to another person and not to them. There is nothing wrong with the question that Manager 1 asks in the example below. It is simply too early to consider someone else's point of view when the subordinate's point of view has not been fully examined. In the beginning the focus is best kept on them. Once you have fully explored the problem as it exists for them *and* have explored their feelings about it and are ready to move on to changing the way they perceive and deal with the problem, then this question would be appropriate.

Subordinate:	'My secretary is always irritable. She is difficult every time I ask her to do something.'

Manager 1:	'Why do you think she is irritable?'
Subordinate:	'Maybe she's having problems at home. She is irritable with other people as well.'
Subordinate:	'My secretary is always irritable. She is difficult every time I ask her to do something.'
Manager 2:	'What effect is this having on you?'
Subordinate:	'It's making me avoid her.'
Manager 2:	'You now prefer not to have contact with her.'
Subordinate:	'Yes, and this is now affecting our work!'

Manager 2's response focuses on the subordinate and the effects the situation is having on them. Talking in this manner will help the subordinate to see that the situation *is* causing a problem for them and that action needs to be taken on *their* part to attempt to remedy it.

Not only do we want to encourage subordinates to acknowledge that they have a problem of their own on their hands, but we may also need to take this a stage further and encourage them to acknowledge that some of their own actions (or inaction) may be supporting or continuing their problem.

SILENCE IS GOLDEN

If counselling skills are used appropriately, there will be silent periods in the conversation. At first, this might make you uncomfortable. Many people are uncomfortable with silence, and feel as if they need to fill it by saying something. When counselling, however, silence actually improves the conversation remarkably. It allows time to consider what has been said, and to gather thoughts and clarify them. Silence also gives time and space to get in touch with thoughts and feelings which are not so immediate and close to the surface. If you talk too much, you block your subordinates from feeling, thinking and talking. Using silence effectively is another way of encouraging them to take responsibility for talking about the real problem. This silent time is not wasted; it is very productive.

Their silence can mean one of many things: thinking about what has been said, or where to go next; sorting out feelings, or just feeling the feelings; wanting you to speak; conveying anger, refusal to engage; not having words to express, blockage or blankness; respect; fear; embarrassment; boredom; sadness; or contempt. If subordinates are silent for a very long time, you can talk to them about what the silence means.

EMOTION

In order to use counselling skills effectively, you need to understand emotions. When subordinates bring problems to you, there are two ways in which emotions can have an effect on the conversation: the subordinate might be in an emotional state to start with, or suddenly have an emotional outburst during the course of the conversation; or they might be repressing emotions in a detrimental way. In the first case, you need to know how to respond to their emotional behaviour, and in the second case you need to address the repressed emotions.

Outbursts and ventilation

When your subordinates are already in or get into an emotional state, you should be aware that they will need a period of time to discharge the emotions (in Phase 1) before moving on either to define or resolve the problem. You have to allow this discharge, often referred to by psychologists as ventilation, to happen. See it as positive because discharging emotion will allow them to move on. Your encouragement of their accepting, expressing and releasing (rather than suppressing) emotions is extremely important and healthy. If emotions are not dealt with, feelings will bubble beneath the surface, and affect the subordinate in detrimental ways, blocking them from proceeding, or showing up as unwanted behaviours.

One problem in our society is shame about showing emotion. Managers tend to think that they are doing the proper and polite thing by ignoring emotions – behaving in a professional manner and saving face for people who might be embarrassed about a display of emotion. This well-intentioned attitude causes a lot of damage because it means that problems are not fully worked through and resolved. Time and time again I have seen delegates on my counselling skills course practise counselling skills in roleplays and make the mistake of ignoring emotions even when the emotions have been clearly verbally expressed. When these delegates stuck to the logical and matter-of-fact problem solving and did not show acknowledgement and understanding of the feelings communicated, then the feelings were repeatedly brought up by the subordinate, sometimes verbally, other times non-verbally, stopping the process from continuing until the feelings were acknowledged.

How should you deal with strong emotions? Allow subordinates to cry – even encourage it. Let them continue crying until the tears subside naturally. Crying is a healthy release of the build-up of tension and stress. Interrupting the crying process is interrupting the restoring process of emotional release. Acknowledge verbally what the person is feeling and let them experience the painful emotions fully. This is what is needed in order for them to move on.

The same is true of other emotions, such as anger. So long as subordinates are not threatening you or company property, allow them to express their anger. While they are expressing strong emotions you may feel at a loss for what to do. The best is to do as little as possible while waiting patiently. Anything you try to discuss while they are in a highly emotional state will not be heard anyway. The only useful comments are reflections of what the subordinate is feeling, and reassurances that their feelings are normal and natural, which show them that you understand and accept their emotions.

Sometimes this discharging of emotion in the presence of an empathetic human being is all that is needed. Afterward the release of emotions is over, the person's mind may be clearer, their will and confidence stronger, and they may be ready to resolve matters on their own.

Other times, seeing subordinates through an initial emotional phase will lead to their being able to express their thoughts in a rational enough manner to begin determining specifically what the problem is and what can be done about it. This is one of the reasons why it is not appropriate for managers to help subordinates with long-term, deep-seated emotional problems. The initial phase of recognising and releasing pent-up emotions will take much more specialist skill and time than a manager has to offer.

Repression

Figure 11.3 shows the interaction between feelings (emotions),

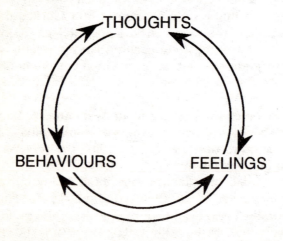

Figure 11.3

thoughts and behaviours. The inner arrow demonstrates the cycle in one direction: feelings affect thoughts which affect behaviours. Thoughts are often expressions of feelings at various levels of awareness. If your subordinate is exhibiting strange or inexplicable behaviours, it may be due to a repressed feeling. For example, belligerent behaviour towards authority figures could be due to a fear of them. The person may not be aware of the feeling (fear), and may not even be conscious of the resulting behaviour (belligerence). Another example is a supervisor's compulsive perfectionism which causes him or her continually to watch over employees' shoulders. The underlying feeling could be inadequacy. Feelings are often displaced onto a safer and easier target. For example, anger towards a dominating partner can be taken out on subordinates. Once the feeling is revealed, acknowledged, expressed and accepted, then the behaviour is likely to lessen. Behind poor performance is often an unexpressed feeling.

When subordinates are avoiding discussing emotions – refusing to acknowledge emotions and talking only on a logical level when you suspect there are indeed emotions involved – then encourage them to talk about the repressed feelings. You can either reflect only the emotional content of their communication, or ask direct questions about what they are feeling.

Positive thinking

The emotions/thoughts/behaviours cycle works in both directions. The outer cycle of arrows illustrates that thoughts also affect feelings, which in turn manifest themselves in behaviours. This cycle in the diagram is very useful for explaining to subordinates the power of positive thinking. People can feel more positive if they change their thoughts. Note that positive thinking tends to work only *after* negative feelings have been validated; otherwise, it just becomes another way of repressing them.

Emotional blocks to taking action

Emotional blocks can impede people from taking action, even when, on a logical level, they want to do so. If there is no apparent reason why your subordinate is not implementing their action plan, then there is likely to be an emotional block which is preventing them from progressing. Try to help them to recognise and work through the block.

Ask them about what thoughts and feelings may be blocking them. For example, you could ask, 'What are you feeling when you consider

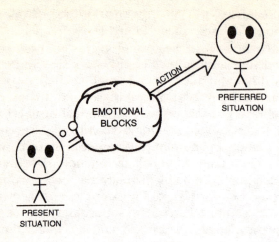

Figure 11.4

doing X?', or 'What thoughts are going through your mind when you imagine trying this option?' Becoming aware of and talking about the blocks will help them to overcome them.

Some common emotional blocks which prevent the necessary action being taken to bring about the desired change include:

■ Fear of failure or of their efforts being wasted.
■ Fear of other people's reactions to their changes.
■ Fear of higher expectations from others – not being able to cope with the new situation.
■ Uncertainty about choice – 'Am I making the right decision?'
■ Difficulty visualising self in new position.
■ Fear of the unknown and risk – known pain (in their present situation) is comfortable because it is predictable.

The change itself can be what is frightening them. People are creatures of habit and somehow comfortable in their present situation, even if they don't like it. People get used to being unhappy, and the fear of trying to change (which leads to a new, unknown situation) can be greater than the fear of remaining unhappy in the present situation. If they do begin to change, they can become frightened of their own strange new feelings which result.

One note of caution: occasionally people get stuck in a rut, remaining in an emotional mode for too long. Once the feelings have been adequately expressed and released, you should encourage them to move on.

INTERPRETING/OVERINTERPRETING

Common mistakes when beginning to use counselling skills often involve overinterpreting, or interpreting too quickly. Reading between the lines and following hunches can usually only be carried out successfully by professional counsellors. Amateur, 'lay' counsellors should only interpret *very* tentatively, putting forward their interpretation as a question, and only when there are definite indicators (body language, tone of voice) as evidence.

The following is an example of interpreting too quickly, and therefore focusing on the wrong topic.

Security Department Head:	'Our security system is extremely out of date. I can't get the guy in charge of purchasing to listen to me. He's hopeless! The cost of investing in a new one is a lot less than the cost of theft. People go unchecked in and out of this building as they please.'
Manager:	'So we are having a problem with theft then.'

The real concern of the security head may be communication with the purchasing department and the process for making purchasing decisions, or it may be a personality conflict with the 'guy in charge of purchasing'. This manager probably interpreted that theft was the important issue because he or she jumped to conclusions too soon. More open questions (which don't lead the conversation yet) and/or listening are needed at this stage to discover which issue is of real concern to the security department head.

Below is a situation where the manager is overinterpreting.

Regional Sales Manager:	'One member of my sales team, Jill, is cleverer than I am. She often wants to rewrite bits of my proposals.'
Product Manager:	'You feel threatened by Jill's intelligence.'

Unless there were previous indications, or telling body language or tone of voice along with the sales manager's statement, this would be overinterpretation. The sales manager did not mention feeling threatened. Maybe he or she feels proud of Jill and her intelligence, and excited about what she can contribute to the sales team.

Your interpretation may or may not be correct. Your subordinate may have a different and legitimate interpretation or explanation. Therefore, interpretations need to be put forward very tentatively, allowing the subordinate plenty of opportunity to modify them. If the sales manager in the last example sounded angry and was physically tense, then a better response to the sales manager above would be: 'You seem a bit anxious. Is it possible that Jill's intelligence is worrying you?'

If there was no indication from the sales manager's voice or body language regarding feelings about Jill's cleverness, then asking a simple question such as 'How do you feel about that?' would be more appropriate.

SYMPTOM OR CAUSE

You should be aware that the original problem as presented by the subordinate is often not a full explanation of the real problem. It could be a symptom of the underlying problem, or it could be totally unrelated, especially if the subordinate feels too uncomfortable to jump straight into talking about the real problem. Sometimes a smaller sub-problem of the bigger, deeper problem is brought up. Be aware that this occurs, and be prepared either to probe, or to offer plenty of space (silence) to let things emerge so that you are sure you have a full picture of the situation before moving on to problem solving. The subordinate is likely to need encouragement, rapport and trust building to go deeper.

Probing carefully will also help to determine what is the best method of problem solving. It is all too easy just to send someone who is struggling on a training course which sounds as if it will cover the general area of the problem. Sending subordinates for training is a very typical attempt to solve their problems. If the training does not address the real issues, however, it can be an expensive error. Using counselling skills can sometimes be more effective (and cost-effective) than a training course. At other times the subordinate's problem is part of a larger organisational problem. Try to uncover and face the real feelings and issues underlying superficial problems.

CASE EXAMPLE 6

Susan was a young applications administrator within a large insurance firm. She had been with the company in this position for eight months and her supervisor, David, was concerned because she was not performing as well as he had expected her to. She did not seem to remember procedures, and was always asking him and colleagues for help with simple tasks. David was puzzled because the work was not difficult, and Susan had performed well during her induction training.

When David met with Susan to chat about how things were going, she expressed no concern or dissatisfaction with her performance. When David mentioned that she seemed to need a lot of help, Susan said that she tended to be a bit forgetful, but that people were always very helpful.

David, annoyed by her requests for help, was tempted to say that he was very concerned about whether Susan was appropriate for a role which required efficiency and organisation and that she needed to pull her socks up. Instead he asked her whether she thought she was happy in the position. She responded that yes she was, but she would prefer to have an assistant to help her. David questioned Susan at length regarding why she should need an assistant when no one in that position before had ever needed one, but got nowhere until Susan finally gave an emotional reason instead of trying to rationalise: 'I suppose it would just be nicer to have someone to work with.' David asked whether Susan had ever worked alone before and it turned out that her previous jobs had all been very social. Susan then realised and admitted that she forgot how to do things so that she would have reasons to go and talk to people.

David's patient and determined questioning got to the underlying problem (loneliness) behind the surface problem (ineffectiveness). He and Susan could then work together to decide how best to manage the real problem (the cause), rather than focusing superficially only on one result (symptom) of that problem.

A WORD OF ADVICE

Do not try to become proficient at all the counselling skills at once. You will be setting yourself up for discouragement and failure. Focus on one skill at a time. Wait until one feels natural, comfortable and effective before moving on to the next. You are likely to get *worse* before you get better! Just keep on going: you will improve. There are four stages which people go through when working on interpersonal skills:

1. **Unconsciously incompetent** You are blissfully unaware of your lack of skill.
2. **Consciously incompetent** You receive some feedback, read a book, take a course, somehow realise that you can improve your skills.

3. **Consciously competent** Things get worse for a while before they get better. You self-consciously struggle to apply what you have learned.

4. **Unconsciously competent** As your new skills become more automatic, they become part of your natural style.

Moving through 2 and 3 is the most difficult transition, but don't give up!

PART IV

Applications

12

Human states

Part IV has been included to provide you with information which will be useful when using counselling skills (this chapter on human states) and to give you ideas regarding situations where counselling skills can be used effectively (Chapters 13 and 14). Each of these topics is the subject of many books and the sections are by no means intended to be complete instructional material. Instead they are designed to stimulate your thoughts with regards to applying counselling techniques in your workplace.

It is important to have an understanding of typical emotional responses, as well as the behavioural responses which result, in order to help subordinates understand what is happening to them. People feel tremendous relief when they discover that their emotional reactions are normal, and this knowledge will help them deal more effectively with their emotions and subsequently to move forward.

LIFE STAGES

People go through life stages in their careers and in their personal lives. Decisions and changes in both these areas will constantly affect one another. You cannot assist employees with their career progression without taking into account their personal context. It is crucial to understand the stages that people tend to move through, and to recognise major transition and decision points.

Following are some useful charts to refer to when helping subordinates put their personal and career development issues into some sort of perspective. The first is a chart of typical career stages and concerns. The second focuses on adult personal development, and the third on stages related to the family.

Table 12.1 *Tasks of major adult development periods*

Age	Stage	Psychological Issues
17–22	Early Adult Transition	Reducing dependency on parental support Exploring the possibilities of the adult world Testing out preliminary identities and life choices
22–28	Early Adult Establishment	Making initial choices and commitments to occupation, relationships and lifestyle Initial development of life goals Establishing relationship with mentor
28–33	Age 30 Transition	Working on limitations and flaws of first life-structure Challenging parental assumptions about life and career Making important new career/life choices or reaffirming old ones
33–38	Settling Down	Building a niche in the world (work, family, community, friendships, interests) Defining personal direction and advancement Becoming own person
38–42	Mid-Life Transition	Taking stock of life so far Coming to terms with own mortality Developing stronger sense of who you are and what you want
42–50	Entering Middle Adulthood	Making crucial choices about who you want to be and what you want to do Taking more realistic world view
50–65	Age 50 Transition to Late Adult Transition	Re-evaluating what you have to offer life Achieving adult, social and civic responsibility Adjusting to retirement

Source: CEPEC, 1992.

Table 12.2 *Life and family stages*

Age	Life Stage/Family Tasks	Psychological Issues
15–22	Adolescence/Single Adult	Developing a self-identity separate from parents and teachers Balancing the need for total independence with need for emotional support from adults
22–30	Young Adulthood Transition/Married Adult	Balancing one's own needs with those of another person in an intimate relationship Making commitments to spouse about lifestyle, family values, child-rearing
30–38	Young Adulthood/ Parent of Young Children	Adjusting to the emotional demands of parenthood Maintaining intimate relationship with spouse in light of children's demands

38–45	Mid-Life Transition/ Parent of adolescents	Reassessing current values and commitments; feeling this might be the last chance to make major changes in life Dealing with ambivalent feelings of love and anger toward adolescent children
45–55	Middle Adulthood/ Parent of Grown Children	Building a deeper relationship with spouse, not focused on children Dealing with feelings of loss, both of children leaving home and of parents ageing or dying
55–62	Late-Life Transition/ Grandparent	Developing new hobbies, activities and friendships that will be more appropriate with a declining work role Helping children cope financially and emotionally with their new family responsibilities
62–70	Late Adulthood/ Grandparent/ Widow(er)	Dealing with increased awareness of death, perhaps brought on by illness or death of spouse Coming to terms with one's life choices

Source: From *Managing Careers in Organisations* by Daniel C Feldman. © 1988 Scott, Foresman and Company. Reprinted with permission of Harper Collins College Publishers.

Table 12.3 *Career stages and career concerns*

Age	Career Stage	Career Tasks	Psychological Issues
15–22	**Pre-Career: Exploration**	Finding the right career Getting the appropriate education	Discovering one's own needs and interests Developing a realistic self-assessment of one's abilities
20–30	**Early Career: Trial**	Getting a viable first job Adjusting to daily work routines and supervisors	Overcoming the insecurity of inexperience; developing self-confidence Learning to get along with others in a work setting
30–38	**Early Career: Establishment**	Choosing a special area of competence Becoming an independent contributor to the organisation	Deciding on level of professional and organisational commitment Dealing with feelings of failure of first independent projects or challenges
38–45	**Middle Career: Transition**	Reassessing one's true career abilities, talents and interests Withdrawing from one's own mentor and preparing to become a mentor to others	Reassessing one's progress relative to one's ambitions Resolving work life/ personal life conflicts

Table 12.3 *Continued*

Age	Career Stage	Career Tasks	Psychological Issues
45–55	**Middle Career: Growth**	Being a mentor Taking on more responsibilities of general management	Dealing with the competitiveness and aggression of younger people on the fast track in the organisation Learning to substitute wisdom-based experience for immediate technical skills
55–62	**Late Career: Maintenance**	Making strategic decisions about the future of the business Becoming concerned with the broader role of the organisation in civic and political arenas	Becoming primarily concerned with the organisation's welfare rather than one's own career Handling highly political or important decisions without becoming emotionally upset
62–70	**Late Career: Withdrawal**	Selecting and developing key subordinates for future leadership roles Accepting reduced levels of power and responsibility	Finding new sources of life satisfaction outside of job Maintaining a sense of self-worth without a job

Source: From *Managing Careers in Organisations* by Daniel C Feldman. © 1988 Scott, Foresman and Company. Reprinted by permission of Harper Collins College Publishers.

CASE EXAMPLE 7

Tim was 45 and worked as a mid-level manager within a large conglomerate. He had worked for this company for 23 years, steadily progressing upwards, and was comfortably established and well respected there. He had recently received a promotion to a position two levels higher, which was going to offer him a lot more responsibility, although in a different section of the organisation. When Tim received notice of his promotion, he was elated and very proud that his service and loyalty were paying off. He excitedly told all his family and friends the news. He was due to begin work in his new role in another month.

As the time to begin his new role approached, however, Tim became more and more apprehensive. He decided to visit his boss, Carol, who, although sorry to lose him, was very pleased for him. Carol was able to see Tim immediately and invited him into her office. He explained how worried he was feeling about moving to the new role. Carol questioned him about his fears and was surprised when Tim talked more about his personal life than about the new role. He said he thought that his wife was not particularly thrilled about his promotion, although she had not said so directly. But he was not clear about exactly what was bothering him. Carol suggested that they meet again in a week to talk more.

During the course of the next discussion it came to light that Tim had really been looking forward to taking it easier at work now and to putting more energy into his hobbies, particularly gardening which was a hobby he shared with his wife. He had only been partially aware that he was being more and more drawn to interests outside work, but became more conscious of this when the excitement regarding his promotion began to be replaced with a feeling of unease. Tim's ambitions were changing, and the promotion opportunity made him realise this, and think about how he wanted to focus his energies in the future. He said that he would prefer to stay in his present position and hoped that the company would be happy to

LIFE SKILLS

There are some basic skills which are necessary in life. When people are struggling, it is often because they are either unskilled or neglecting their skills in a certain area. Suggested areas where subordinates may need improvement include:

- Managing feelings.
- Thinking processes.
- Relationships.
- Education/learning.
- Relaxation/leisure.
- Time management.
- Health.

TRANSITION PHASES

When people go through a major transition, especially one which has been suddenly thrust on them rather than chosen and anticipated (eg redundancy, death of someone close), there are feelings which are commonly experienced, often in the order shown below (Kubler-Ross, 1975).

1. **Immobilization** Sense of being overwhelmed, frozen, unable to make plans.
2. **Minimisation** Trivialising the change or disruption, denying the magnitude of its effects.
3. **Depression** Realities of the change become apparent. Feelings of powerlessness, loss of control especially of one's emotions as depression sets in.

4. **Accepting reality** Process of unhooking from the past and preparing to face the future. A clear letting go of the past is important. Becoming more optimistic.
5. **Testing** Beginning to test out the new situation – trying new behaviours, lifestyles, and new ways of coping. Will probably be fragile – easily angered and irritable.
6. **Search for meaning** Following the testing period, concern with understanding the changes, seeking meaning for how things are different and why they are different.
7. **Internalisation** Integrating meaning into developing adaptive behaviour. Results in personal growth.

Because people are unique and react in their own particular way, not everyone will go through all these stages. You need to be aware of them, however, as you can then help people to understand their reactions. Sometimes people will get stuck at one stage or encounter a problem and slip backwards, and you will need to help them to move on.

Figure 12.1 shows how people's level of self-esteem changes throughout the stages.

BEREAVEMENT/GRIEVING

The death of a loved one is one of the most difficult unchosen

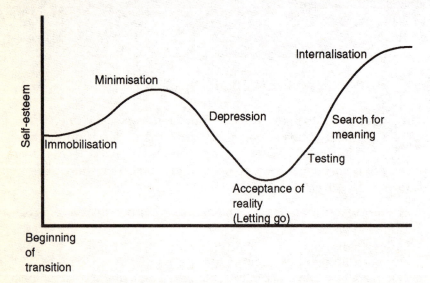

Figure 12.1 *Self-esteem changes during transitions*

Source: Kubler-Ross, 1975.

transitions most people will face. But it is important to remember that people go through a grieving period over other losses as well: job, home, self-respect, body part or body function, lost expectations. In order to aid their adjustment, encourage your subordinates to talk about their loss, and to experience their pain rather than to suppress it.

If subordinates are grieving over something which is difficult, but not terribly traumatic (eg a lost expected promotion or another job- or career-related loss) and you want to help them to move out of denial, a useful approach is to reflect back their statements of denial and then add on a statement which indicates the opposite. For example, for a staff member whose largest client has changed over from your company to a new supplier you could say: 'You say you are hoping to convince Tom to hire us again, yet he has made it clear verbally, and twice in writing, that the decision to use Competitor X is final. Is it likely that he will change his mind now?' You could also challenge by asking the subordinate where their time is better spent – chasing Tom to change his mind, or chasing new business.

Note that the counselling skills of challenging and confronting are *not* recommended for managers helping people suffering from the death of loved ones, lost body parts, or other very serious losses. All a manager can do for someone who is grieving over a very traumatic loss is to listen and reflect, reassure, and refer them for professional help if they appear to need more counselling or support. Reassuring subordinates will be easier if you have some knowledge of normal emotional and physical responses to bereavement.

Common feelings experienced include:

- shock/numbness;
- depression;
- despair;
- longing;
- anger/resentment;
- hopelessness;
- fear;
- helplessness;
- loneliness;
- guilt;
- worthlessness.

Common physical symptoms include:

- insomnia;
- inability to concentrate/forgetfulness;
- breathing problems;

- exhaustion;
- gastro-intestinal problems;
- loss of appetite;
- general ill-health.

STRESS

Employee stress is one of the largest problems facing organisations today. Anxiety is one of the main causes of poor performance at work. Having a general understanding of stress will help you to assist anxious subordinates. This section is intended to be a very simple framework to assist you in recognising stress symptoms in subordinates, and in being knowledgeable about both the sources of stress and effective versus ineffective ways of coping with it.

First, it is important to understand that the sources of stress vary from person to person. What is stressful to one person may not be at all to another. Individuals vary not only in their perceptions of stressors, but also in their skills in managing stress and in their confidence to change and cope. Remember also that a certain manageable level of stress is positive and motivating.

Signs of overstress in subordinates include, according to the British Association for Counselling (BAC):

- loss in productivity or performance;
- high level of lateness, sickness or absenteeism;
- high level of errors or accidents;
- uncooperative behaviour;
- excessive anger at minor irritations;
- clashes with colleagues;
- an obvious level of tension or anxiety;
- a fatigued, weary or despondent air;
- inability to focus on the job at hand;
- hyperactivity;
- inability to slow down or relax;
- lack of care for personal appearance.

Human beings have instinctive reactions to negative stress, called the 'fight or flight' responses. These responses may be helpful for animals whose territories have been invaded, but at work people are often in a situation where neither is beneficial. The unhealthy symptoms of stress result from the body being put repeatedly into a danger-alert state, prepared to 'fight or flee', without any release.

Physical problems which result from continued overstress include:

- fatigue;
- tensed muscle groups;
- insomnia;
- operating in high-speed 'overdrive';
- early heart attacks or heart disease;
- migraines and tension headaches;
- back pain;
- damage to the immune system;
- gastric and intestinal ulcers;
- hypertension.

Mental symptoms include:

- clouded judgement;
- impaired concentration;
- rigid behaviour patterns;
- low motivation;
- low confidence and self-esteem;
- poor communication;
- low trust in others;
- isolation – lack of involvement with work colleagues;
- lack of concern for achievement.

Sources of stress can be either internal (from within the individual) or external (from the individual's environment), or a mixture of both. There can also be either temporary or ongoing problems which cause stress. Stress which is external comes from the environment or organisation, and stress which is internal has to do with the individual's ability to cope with demands placed on them.

Problems which are often (but not always) external include:

- Too much change at once.
- Important changes which come as a surprise.
- Work overload (either too much to do, or too difficult to do).
- Work underload (boredom and too little stimulation are also stressful).
- Insufficient information for job to be performed effectively.
- Conflicts in demands placed on the person.
- Unrealistic objectives or time pressures.
- Organisation has poor internal communications.
- Incompetent senior management.
- Organisation weak in structure and procedures.
- Organisation/culture/manager overly authoritarian or bureaucratic.
- Feeling of not being able to make a difference.
- Difficult relationship with boss or subordinates.

- Difficult relationships with colleagues (competition, not being able to share problems).
- Being unable to control, contain or remedy a situation.
- Important goals are made inaccessible.
- Regular but unpredictable crises (creating a state of negative expectation which is exhausting).
- Tedious work.
- Interruptions.
- Role conflict.
- Values, interests, or aims conflicting with others.
- Lack of personal control over things important to the person.

The graph of difficulty/ability zones in Figure 12.2 is a useful visual representation for discussing work difficulty with subordinates. It demonstrates how competence in any specific context will depend on the relationship between two perceptions: that of the perceived difficulty of the task and the perceived ability to achieve it (Elliot, 1993).

1. **Panic zone**   Here the task is perceived to be well above the ability to achieve it. The reaction will probably be panic, anxiety and stress. Avoidance is likely and incompetent performance very likely.
2. **Stretch zone**   The work expected is just a little more than the subordinate thinks they can achieve. It poses a challenge, releases energy, and engenders a sense of achievement.

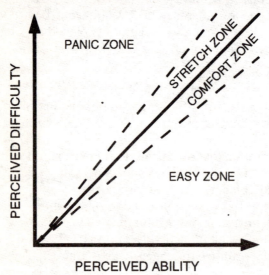

Figure 12.2   *Difficulty/Ability Zones*

Source: *Personnel Today*.

3. **Comfort zone**   The work is difficult enough to be challenging, yet within the subordinate's perceived ability to do it. Tasks are approached with zest and confidence.
4. **Easy zone**   The work appears easy and well within the subordinate's competence. Reaction may be boredom or lack of concentration.

Problems which are often internal include:

- Fear of being promoted and dealing with the new responsibilities.
- Lack of skill in interacting with people.
- Lack of confidence or low self-esteem.
- Inner fears and anxieties.
- Inability to listen.
- Fear of not being promoted or not meeting other goals.
- Anxiety about abilities.
- Being alone without support.
- Emotional overload (taking on other people's problems).

Once the sources of stress have been identified, then an important decision must be made: whether to remove or change the stressor (if possible), or whether to change the reactive coping mechanism(s). First the subordinate needs to analyse the situations to decide what is changeable and what is not. Managing stress means consciously monitoring our personal reactions to life; that is, learning how to cope positively (both in our thinking and in our behaviour) to change, other people, conflict, pressures, etc.

Positive ways of coping with stress are usually ones in which the subordinate tries to take control of the situation (attempting to affect either the stressor or the reaction), whereas negative ways of coping are usually attempts to avoid a situation (avoid the stressor or avoid/ repress the reaction). It generally feels better to do something about a situation than to feel like a victim running or hiding. But sometimes attempting to control the situation is not a good idea, and avoiding is not such a bad idea.

Coping strategies which are usually positive include:

- Trying to find out more about the situation.
- Social support (sharing problems with others).
- Trying to see the positive side of the situation.
- Making a plan of action and following it.
- Taking things one day at a time, one step at a time.
- Trying to step back from the situation and be more objective.
- Trying not to act too hastily or follow the first hunch.
- Learning how to relax.
- Constructive self-talk.

- Improving diet.
- Challenging cognitive distortion.
- Changing aggressive or passive behaviour.
- Balancing lifestyle.
- Leisure time use.
- Time management.
- Relaxation training (biofeedback, meditation, etc).
- Emotional outlets (professional counselling, writing it out).
- Physical activities (exercise, sports, muscular relaxation, stamina building).

Coping strategies which are usually negative include:

- Taking problems/stress out on other people.
- Keeping feelings to self.
- Isolating (avoiding being with people).
- Denial.
- Alcohol.
- Overeating.
- Tranquillising or recreational drugs.
- Psychological withdrawal (breakdowns).
- Self-delusion (distorting reality).
- Inappropriate humour.

By using counselling skills with stressed subordinates, you can help them to turn negative responses of anxiety, fear, confusion and indecision into challenge, opportunity and effort. Help them to determine their sources of stress, and their ways of coping, and to generate alternatives.

Organisational interventions to help employees with stress are often focused on the individual, and concentrate on modifying employees' reactions to stressful situations or counselling for personal problems. There is, however, another level at which intervention is required, which is addressing aspects of job and organisational design to find out where unproductive stress is generated and then to redesign these areas.

DEPRESSION

Depression can be due to biochemical or pyschological causes.

1. **Acute depression** Caused by negative events such as illness, bereavement, divorce, a period of continuous stress, or postnatal depression.
2. **Organic depression** Due to medication, brain chemistry.

3. **Chronic depression** Caused by long-term blocked anger or
    pain. Depression is a normal result of past anger which someone
    refuses to recognise or acknowledge. Because these are deeper
    causes they are much more difficult to determine. The sub-
    ordinate may not know themselves why they feel depressed, and
    they may not want to talk about it.

As a manager, your counselling skills will be useful in talking to
someone with acute depression, although professional assistance is
also advisable. Talking about the situation and realising its temporary
nature can bring about some reassurance. But anyone whom you
suspect has biochemical or chronic depression should be referred
to a professional (general practitioner, employee assistance programme, or independent counselling organisation). An awareness of
the difference between chronic, organic and acute depression will
make you consider them all as possible reasons for depressive
behaviour, and give you a framework for thinking about when to
suggest that your subordinates seek professional help.

13

Performance management

The term 'performance management' is often used to describe a re-vamped appraisal system or a performance-related bonus scheme. Performance management, however, needs to be looked at in the much larger and more comprehensive context of continuous improvement in business performance. The 'holistic' performance management system takes into account several ongoing and integrated processes, within the framework of achieving overall business strategy. Most of these processes involve the use of counselling skills.

Figure 13.1 shows the interrelated nature of the aspects of performance management. Setting objectives leads to determining what human resources are needed to meet the objectives, and what supports and resources these staff will need to meet their individual objectives. Then achievement and progress need to be assessed, both formally and informally. The cycle continues as new objectives are planned and decisions are made regarding how to allocate human resources in the future.

Once the system is going, the aspects become interrelated, feeding back and forth to one another. For example, appraisal gives rise to new training and support requirements as well as vice versa, and appraisals give rise to new objectives as well as assessing how well old ones were met. Manpower planning decisions such as recruitment and redundancy instigate new training or counselling needs, and the growth that arises from supporting and developing people engenders the need for succession planning and monetary rewards. All the aspects must work together, with continuous feedback to one another, in order for the system to work.

The performance management system promotes self-improvement at both the level of the individual and of the organisation. Thus each aspect of the performance management system

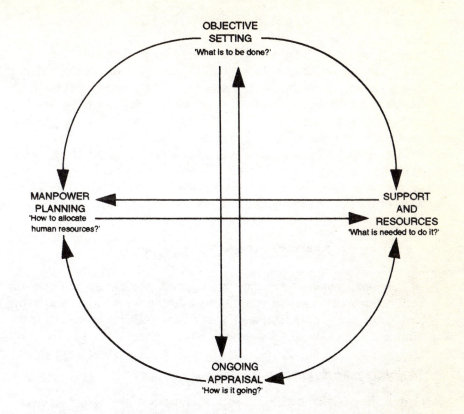

Figure 13.1 *Performance management system*

must be considered at both these levels. Objectives are set at the level of the organisation (strategies) as well as at the level of the individual (how the individual will contribute to the strategies). Human resource requirements are considered relative to the company's needs to promote, downsize, transfer or recruit, and on the individual level, where career aspirations are taken into account. Resources and support for achieving objectives must be procured for the company (information and communication technology, building space usage, large-scale training programmes etc) as well as for individuals who will have their own specific training, resources, coaching and counselling requirements. Appraisal must also take place at both levels, monitoring both organisational and individual capability.

The following sections discuss how counselling skills are used at the individual level within the different processes of the performance management system.

SETTING OBJECTIVES

There are two main areas of opportunity for using counselling skills when setting objectives. First, while corporate and departmental objectives will usually be determined by management (with or without employee input), your counselling skills can be used to encourage your subordinates to think about how they are going to contribute to meeting the objectives. Secondly, you can use counselling skills to help your subordinates come up with additional objectives of their own, as well as plans for meeting them. Counselling skills may also be helpful in getting subordinates to suggest ways of measuring their progress and performance.

SUPPORT AND RESOURCES

In this aspect of performance management there are the obvious applications of counselling skills to training, coaching, mentoring and counselling subordinates. There is another area worth mentioning in more detail – training needs analysis.

Training needs analysis

Counselling skills can be used to pinpoint the exact areas of developmental requirements, as well as for determining which modes of support will be most useful. For example, if your subordinate needs to improve their supervisory skills, then you can use counselling skills to determine more precisely what exactly their difficulties are, and which particular supervisory skills are weak. Then you can use counselling skills to determine whether a training course, coaching or counselling will be most helpful, or some combination of these. Too often the response to a developmental need is to send the subordinate on a course that sounds as if it will cover the topic. Using your counselling skills will help you to ascertain the exact nature and depth of the need, and to determine together a method of learning which will be most suited to that need.

HUMAN RESOURCE PLANNING

An organisation's human resource planning should be performed alongside career planning for individuals. The supply and demand of human resources are matched so that skills are utilised to the best possible advantage, and the aspirations of the individual are taken into account. This coordination of organisational and individual needs is becoming more common as companies recognise that they have to make the best use of human resources and that staff turnover is expensive. This component of human resource planning is referred to as succession planning.

Counselling skills will be useful during the part of the succession planning process which involves talking to your subordinates; in other words, during career counselling.

Career counselling

Career counselling is a specialist form of counselling, and indeed a career in itself. As a manager, you will only be involved in career counselling peripherally and you are likely to have difficulty remaining neutral regarding your subordinates' decision making. However, if you can work with subordinates to help them achieve their own goals as well as company objectives, they will be much more happy and productive.

Career counselling involves looking at alternatives and making choices in order to get people from where they are at present to where they want to be. Although you may not be able to assist them regarding career opportunities outside the firm, you can provide information about opportunities and options which exist within the firm, and help them with self-assessment, generating realistic alternatives, and decision making:

- Provide information:
  — job descriptions;
  — personal qualities and educational levels necessary for jobs;
  — realistic estimates of future organisational requirements;
  — resources for further information.
- Assist in self-assessment:
  — general abilities;
  — special aptitudes;
  — strengths and weaknesses;
  — interests and job needs.
- Assist in generating options.
- Assist in the decision-making process:
  — short-term;
  — long-term.

Career counselling will take different slants depending on the stage the subordinates are at in their careers. Early career issues involve finding one's area of contribution, learning how to fit into the organisation, becoming productive, and seeing a viable future for oneself in the career. Mid-career issues involve choosing an aspect and building one's career around it (specialising vs. generalising). Late career issues involve becoming a mentor, using one's experience and wisdom, letting go and retiring.

APPRAISAL

The most effective appraisals meet subordinates' needs, as well as those of the manager and the organisation. In addition to being opportunities to assess, develop and motivate, appraisals are an opportunity for subordinates to pursue their own issues and concerns.

Appraisals will have one or more of the following objectives:

1. To provide feedback on performance by giving subordinates information and assessment on achievements and results:
   — praise;
   — formal assessment of unsatisfactory performance.
2. To ask subordinates how they view their performance.
3. To review the job to see if there is a better way of carrying it out.
4. To set new objectives and targets.
5. To improve performance.
6. To determine future potential and discuss career development opportunities and plans.
7. To assess training and development needs:
   — identifying strengths and weaknesses;
   — identifying how to improve skills.
8. To plan future promotions, pay, and successions.
9. To motivate staff:
   — positive feedback on objectives achieved and personal strengths;
   — suggestions for improvement;
   — setting personal targets – giving people direction and something to aim for.
10. To provide a fair standard for comparison.
11. Communication – to provide an opportunity for constructive conversation between manager and subordinates.

The skills required for conducting an appraisal include obtaining information, providing feedback, problem solving, motivating and counselling. Depending on the nature of the appraisal, these skills will be used in varying degrees, but all of the objectives above can best be achieved by using counselling skills to some degree.

There is a current trend towards emphasising the future in appraisals. The process is less likely to be a manager's assessment of a subordinate's past performance, as was common in the past. Instead, appraisals are now more likely to be mutually participative, which leads to a greater 'ownership' of the outcome on the part of subordinates, and therefore makes them more likely to improve. The most effective way to do an appraisal is to focus it mainly on the subordinate, that is, to get the subordinate to do as much of it as possible themselves, which is synonymous with the counselling style. This is idealistic in some cases, however. Although you want the appraisal to be as objective a process as possible, it is impossible to have no judgements or opinions involved. Nevertheless, since the success of the appraisal is very dependent on your subordinate's perception of its fairness, it is important to elicit and consider their thoughts. If appraisal schemes are not handled well, they can be worse than useless in that they can actually worsen both performance and working relationships.

One way to increase perceptions of the fairness of appraisals is to rate everyone in similar positions along the same criteria. Another way is to use your counselling skills to persuade subordinates to air their views and concerns.

Specific areas in which counselling skills will help you to do an appraisal include:

1. Putting the subordinate at ease if their body language indicates tension.
2. Being aware of both your own and the subordinate's likely feelings, which will help you to establish rapport at the beginning (de Board, 1983):
   — *Manager*
      (a) Positive feelings:
         ■ To be helpful and understanding.
         ■ To be kind and tolerant.
      (b) Negative feelings:
         ■ Fear of carrying out the interview ineffectively.
         ■ Fear of unleashing powerful emotions.
   — *Subordinate*
      (a) Positive feelings:
         ■ To be liked and accepted.
         ■ To get help with problems.
      (b) Negative feelings:
         ■ Fear of criticism and punishment.
3. Giving subordinates advance warning of appraisals, requesting them to think ahead about certain topics, will help them to feel

more prepared and confident and more aware of what to expect.

4. Getting the subordinate to volunteer as much information as possible and then probing areas that they don't cover. Some subordinates may want your point of view instead (the 'that is what managers are paid for' attitude) but they are in the minority compared to people who would prefer to assess and criticise themselves constructively. People are sensitive to criticism from others and tend to reject it, even when it is justified and there is valid proof or evidence. Operating in a counselling style (trying to get the other person to bring up and discuss their weaknesses) is often much more effective in getting them to consider seriously and accept areas which need improvement. A neutral scale on paper which you can both work from is a useful device to have. Figure 13.2 is a sample of such a scale, using teamwork as an example.

If the main objectives of the appraisal are to enhance the sub-

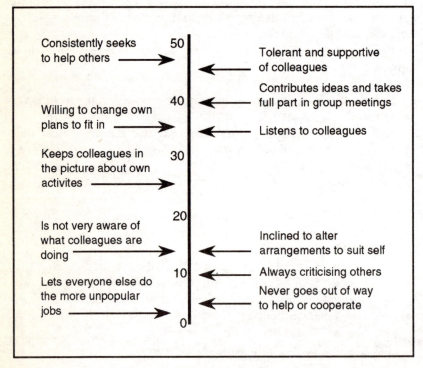

Figure 13.2

Source: This figure is taken from *Appraisal: Routes to Improved Performance* by Clive Fletcher, published by the Institute of Personnel and Development and reproduced with their permission.

ordinate's motivation and development, then counselling skills must be used as much as possible. If the objective is to pass on information about poor performance, or to explain why a promotion is not to be given, then counselling skills are necessary to help the subordinate determine how to improve or move forward once the feedback has been given.

The following are some suggested open questions to commence a counselling style conversation:

- How might you perform more effectively?
- What are the ways of going about this improvement?
- What are your development needs?
- What solutions do you recommend?
- How can we work together more effectively to improve your performance?
- Describe the situations where your job goes well.
- Describe the situations where your job does not go well.
- What aspects of the job are difficult?
- What objectives have not been met?
- What changes or challenges are likely to occur in the near future?
- Where do you feel satisfied with your efforts? (Ask for examples.)
- Where do you not feel satisfied with your efforts? (Ask for examples.)
- What are your career aspirations? – aims, interests, changes since our last discussion/new aspects.
- What are your feelings about the position and your future potential?

As with any counselling situation, follow-up is a very important aspect of appraisals. The meeting must produce a basis for future action. Following it up shows subordinates that their conversation has been taken seriously and that an appraisal is meaningful, not just a formality.

Another important trend is operating an ongoing appraisal process which consists of three components: regular feedback regarding day-to-day operations, periodic meetings in order to keep up to date, proactive regarding the broader and longer-term context; and formal annual appraisals for record keeping and managerial decision making. Rather than waiting until the formal appraisal time rolls around, counselling skills can be used in continuing assessment, communication and trouble-shooting processes.

Other areas in which counselling skills are involved in managing performance are during pre-disciplinary meetings and grievance interviews.

PRE-DISCIPLINARY ACTION

The term *pre*-disciplinary is used because the use of counselling skills is not a substitute for disciplinary action. Instead, the use of counselling skills precedes and is complementary to disciplinary action. Using counselling techniques at an earlier stage before initiating disciplinary action can often prevent the need for that action; using counselling skills along with the formal disciplinary procedure can help subordinates to take ownership of and responsibility for resolving the problem.

Personal problems, of course, should be allowed to remain private unless the person is willing to talk or the problem is adversely affecting their work. In fact, managers may feel uncomfortable about initiating a conversation with a subordinate whose work has not yet been very adversely affected by their problem. However, if attempting to tackle the problem early might avoid its getting much worse, then giving it a try is worthwhile.

CASE EXAMPLE 8

A normally polite and pleasant customer service representative was known to have a personal problem which was making him edgy and sharper than usual when dealing with people.This developed to the stage where his approach to the customer became unacceptable and the first steps of discipline had to be taken. A counselling session set up by the individual's manager or supervisor when an enduring problem first became apparent would perhaps have prevented more drastic steps.

Example adapted from: *The Skills of Interviewing* (1988) by Leslie Rae.

If your offer is rejected, do not push the subordinate. Simply point out that the situation cannot be allowed to continue indefinitely if it is having a negative effect on the company, and then continue to monitor performance. You can offer help again later on.

Pre-disciplinary counselling sessions fall into different categories – sometimes you have the facts, and at other times you have to do investigatory work. If you have the facts then you need first to communicate the problem clearly and concisely. Then use your counselling skills to try to establish agreement on the existence of the problem, and to help the person to decide on courses of action. If you ask too many questions before sharing your reasons for the meeting, you will appear furtive.

Pre-disciplinary counselling sessions are difficult because of the emotional content. In response to your statement of the problem(s), you are likely to get an emotional outburst, denial of a problem, or deflections away from your point.

Use your counselling skills to listen to the person's emotional outburst and let them take their time. Acknowledge their feelings and reflect back the emotional content. Do not make any judgements about their feelings: not 'you are right or wrong for feeling upset/angry', just 'you are upset/angry about that'. In order to avoid getting caught up in deflections, you need to have a very clear idea of what the issue is and be sure to keep coming back to it.

Reflection can also be used in a pre-disciplinary situation to play back any ridiculous statements that subordinates make in defense of themselves. Often they will then admit they are not being straight-forward. For example, if a subordinate with an absenteeism problem brings up her new puppy when you refer to her attendance record, you could say, 'Your puppy has stopped you from coming to work regularly over the past few months?' Then she is likely to realise what a weak excuse it sounded.

GRIEVANCE

When a subordinate comes to you with a grievance, you can use a mixture of investigatory and counselling skills to get to the heart of the matter. If you treat the situation completely logically without using counselling skills (for example, 'just give me the facts') then you might miss important information, and you also miss an opportunity to help the subordinate possibly to resolve the situation by a method other than following a formal grievance procedure. Sometimes after talking through a situation with a sympathetic listener, a subordinate will want to go away and think again about how to handle the situation.

14

Organisational applications

LONG-TERM THINKING

A manager who uses counselling skills effectively will address problems when early warning signs become apparent, and will encourage people to come to him or her with problems before they become major issues, thus making the department run more smoothly in the long term. Managers will also benefit from approaching problems which appear to be completely personal and not work related. It is not possible for employees totally to separate their work lives from their outside lives and outside problems *do* eventually have an effect on work performance.

CHANGE MANAGEMENT

In order to create and maintain competitive advantage, companies have to be flexible about changing, and yet continuously uphold the highest level of performance and productivity from employees. Implementing positive strategies to ease the pressures of upheaval and uncertainty is absolutely necessary. Given people's resistance to and natural fear of change, managing it is not an easy task. Employees require counselling to cope with and adjust to changes.

Managers should use counselling skills not only to support and motivate subordinates during periods of change, but also to create the environment towards which organisations are attempting to change. Many companies are benefiting from changing from being downwardly operating, hierarchical, directive and slow to change to being upwardly operating, flatter, facilitative and more flexible. Using counselling skills is essential in order to *implement* this cultural change effectively (rather than just giving it lip service), so an ideal time to institute the top-down training of managers in counselling skills is as part of a change management programme.

DOWNSIZING

Handling the process of downsizing in the most humane manner possible is worthwhile both for the sake of the organisation and for those made redundant. When a large number of people are made redundant, there will be counselling needs at many levels. Besides the redundant employees, others who will need help include the employees remaining and the managers who must communicate the changes and then adjust to running a new organisational structure.

Taking steps to make sure that the remaining staff stay motivated and committed will improve their morale and reassure them that the company cares about them. It preserves the internal company image. Immediately following a large-scale redundancy is an opportune time to institute top-down training of managers in counselling skills. Feelings which are likely to need to be dealt with by using counselling skills include resistance, lack of trust, anger, fear, demotivation, disinterest, hostility, and a disinterest in the future.

MENTORING

Mentoring programmes pair more senior people in the organisation with people who are junior, in order to help them to learn the ropes, advance, and grow and achieve in their career. Mentors help mentees with personal objectives and effectiveness, self-confidence and self-awareness as they apply to organisational objectives, directly or indirectly. The role involves a mixture of counselling, coaching and advising.

The mentor–mentee relationship is less directive than the manager–subordinate relationship. Within the mentoring relationship, mentors are less concerned with their own and departmental objectives, and less worried about loss of professionalism. Subordinates may want to 'paint the best possible picture' for their manager, who is their immediate boss and can affect their pay cheque. They are more likely to open up to a mentor. Successes and failures, personal strengths and weaknesses, and problem areas and difficulties can be discussed and analysed in a relationship which feels safe. Therefore effective counselling skills are especially vital for a mentor.

Services that mentors provide include:

- Helping the mentee to understand how the organisation works.
- Helping the mentee to understand organisational politics.
- Providing specific knowledge about the broader aspects of the business and the industry.
- Helping the mentee to set development goals.
- Helping the mentee to achieve full potential within the organisation.
- Helping the mentee to explore and identify learning needs.
- Determining with the mentee ways of meeting those needs.
- Acting as a neutral and non-judgemental sounding board for new ideas.
- Providing coaching in particular skills.

MANAGING DIVERSITY

Employees are adapting to much more heterogeneous work environments (race, class, sex, religion and culture). Using counselling skills is a way to 'manage diversity'. Adopting a counselling style of management will set an example of how to communicate, learn from one another, and get the most from everyone.

EQUAL OPPORTUNITIES

The use of counselling skills can be invaluable in organisations which are implementing equal opportunity policies. It can assist in tapping and developing the resources of female employees, and also in helping men and women to adjust to one another and work together most productively.

Women may require counselling as they move up the ladders, often alone, into uncharted territory with few role models. Women have not been conditioned for the traditional work environment in the same way that men have been. Counselling can help to provide them with much needed support and confidence.

However, women's conditioning can help them to excel as managers using counselling skills in a modern, cooperative work environment. Men may require counselling in order to adapt to organisational cultures which are becoming less patriarchal and masculine. In the past to get to the top you had to repress feelings, adapt to hierarchy, even deny reality. Emotions were not shown at work, and certainly not discussed. Counselling can help men to break out of old habits and thinking which could hold them back in a modern enviroment.

PRE-RETIREMENT COUNSELLING

Retirement is a major life transition. Because retirement will be such a significant change in lifestyle, it is worthwhile for employees to prepare for it in advance. Individual counselling (or counselling for couples) can be offered as a complement to a group educational programme. There are likely to be issues that people will prefer to discuss privately.

Retirement counselling is best offered by specially trained professionals. However, some employees will want to talk to their managers about the approaching retirement, so having an understanding of what happens during retirement counselling is useful.

Retirement counselling should relieve employees' negative thoughts, build their confidence and be informative. The employee's feelings should be discussed in order to help them to accept the change and its losses, and to anticipate the future in the most positive light. Not enough people realise what an opportunity retirement can be.

Some people look forward to reaching retirement age. Positive feelings about retirement include:

- freedom from demands of work and parenting;
- opportunity to expand on favourite hobby;
- opportunity to try something new;
- more time to spend with family.

Other people dread retirement. Signs of apprehension about retirement are depression or tiredness. Negative feelings about retirement include:

- loss of identity and status;
- lack of purpose/usefulness in life;
- awareness of negative attitudes towards older people;
- loss of income;
- lack of friends outside present work;
- boredom;
- concern about future health.

Providing the employee with information on what to expect (normal reactions to the transition) is helpful. Retired people will often go through three stages as they adjust to their new lifestyle: initially a honeymoon phase, then approximately 6 to 12 months later a period of disenchantment, followed by reorientation and stability (Berry-man, 1991).

TEAM MANAGEMENT/CONFLICT RESOLUTION

Counselling skills can be used very effectively to facilitate groups in problem solving, decision making and conflict resolution. Group counselling is similar to facilitation, but there is more focus on feelings and emotions. It can greatly improve the way teams work together.

When individual project team members suffer from personal problems which affect their ability to work, other team members' ability to work is often affected as well. Sometimes a team will have difficulty working together generally, even where there are not one or two individual problem-causers.

A manager or consultant trained in counselling skills can use a counselling process to address these situations. Someone outside the team has no investment in the work or the outcome, and will be freer to offer interpretations about the group process (the way the team interacts) and to help the team clearly define and communicate expectations. Following are some of the aspects of group process which can be addressed (Kolb, Rubin and McIntyre, 1984):

1. Goals or mission:
   — How clearly defined are the goals?
   — Who sets the goals?
   — How much agreement is there among members concerning the goals? How much commitment?
   — How clearly measurable is goal achievement?
   — How do group goals relate to broader organisational goals? To personal goals?
2. Group norms.
3. Leadership.
4. Decision making:
   — How does it happen?
   — Is everyone satisfied with how it happens?
   — Is there a better way?
5. Role expectations:
   — Role ambiguity – Are people clear about their own and others' roles within the team?
   — Role conflict – Do any team members feel pulled in different directions due to dual or multiple roles?
   — Role overload – Are the responsibilities of the roles man-ageable?

When using counselling skills with teams it is necessary to encourage group members to speak up about their feelings, even when those feelings are vague and unfocused and people feel unsure about them. Insist that the participants listen to one another and try to get them to use 'I' statements to express their own feelings rather than make accusations.

CRISIS/TRAUMA

A crisis is defined as a situation of excessive stress. The frequency of violent and traumatic crises in the workplace is unfortunately increasing. Examples of workplace traumas include accidents leading to serious injury or death, bombs, theft/hold-ups, fire, raids, kidnappings, extortion, floods and other natural disasters.

People who have been involved in or exposed to a traumatic event experience a range of symptoms:

- Shock.
- Unexpected frightening thoughts or visions.
- Nightmares.
- Loss of interest in everyday life.
- Inability to concentrate.
- Insomnia.
- General depression.
- General anxiety.
- Disorientation.
- Fears of insanity or nervous breakdown.

The effects from trauma last much longer than is realised. Often people will attempt to conceal their symptoms. For example, thinking about what *could* have happened is often very disturbing, but people are likely to be reluctant to share this with others at work.

Managers will want to get back to business as usual as quickly as possible. However, if the employees involved are not treated in a considerate manner because managers are unaware of post-traumatic stress syndrome, then the resulting inconsiderate treatment can add to the trauma. Taking time to support traumatised employees will make the return to normal happen much faster.

Experienced trauma counsellors should be summoned when a severe crisis occurs. Their specialist knowledge of trauma and its effects will allow them to recognise people's states and identify those who are severely traumatised. However, whether or not professionals are called in, it is useful for managers to have some knowledge regarding post-traumatic stress syndrome which they can apply.

CONSULTING

In many industries, counselling skills are extremely useful for working with clients as well as with subordinates. Of course, as a consultant you can't use a counselling style completely (usually you have been hired to give answers), but you can use counselling, listening and questioning skills when interviewing to get as much 'real' information as possible, and you can use counselling skills after presenting your expertise and findings to help your client to find ways of using what you have presented.

ENTREPRENEURISM/INTRAPRENEURISM

Venture capitalists, bankers, small business and business start-up consultants, and managers whose subordinates are intrapreneurs (managing start-up ventures within the organisation) can all benefit from applying counselling skills to help the entre- or intrapreneur. Developing and guiding entrepreneurs requires a balance of high support levels along with a high level of challenge. Using counselling skills makes this balance achievable.

The concept of the person's 'ownership' of the business idea, plan or problem resolution is especially applicable to entrepreneurs who tend to see their business as 'their baby' and have difficulty accepting outside advice.

1. Use listening skills to build trust and get them to open up, and to detect problem areas which they may be initially reluctant to reveal.
2. Challenge in a pulling fashion in order to get them to consider rather than defend. Also use counselling skills to help them to take action when they are blocked.
3. Work through decision-making and problem-solving processes with entrepreneurs, so that they can then continue to use these themselves and with their own subordinates.

UPWARD FEEDBACK

Upward feedback is feedback from subordinates regarding their managers' performance. It involves establishing two-way communication, and respecting subordinates by listening, valuing and considering their input. However, upward feedback is difficult for managers and supervisors to receive. The best way to manage this sensitive situation is for the manager or supervisor's own manager to talk about the issues which arise from upward feedback in a counselling style.

It is useful to use an upward feedback software system, where subordinates' appraisal, the manager's own self-appraisal, and your appraisal as his or her manager can all be viewed along each dimension on a chart or graph. The manager being assessed can be asked to comment on the data.

THE LEARNING ORGANISATION

According to *The Learning Organisation Journal*, a learning organisation is 'an organisation which facilitates the learning of all its members and thus continually transforms itself.' A learning organisation therefore aims for continuous business improvement. Learning organisations adopt a very dynamic management style, building a culture which encourages *all* employees to develop and learn.

This book has discussed how you can use counselling skills to develop individuals. The same concepts and skills can be used at team, department and organisational (senior management) levels to encourage self-responsibility for growth, learning, problem solving etc, in order continually to develop the company.

ORGANISATIONAL DEVELOPMENT

In order for an organisation to develop, effective training in counselling skills will need to be introduced as a normal part of its mainstream management development programme. In order for the subsequent use of counselling skills to be effective, however, the company culture must really support the use of these skills, that is, *really* value its people. Otherwise the skills will be used manipulatively, which causes even more underlying problems.

Every organisation has an unstated culture consisting of unwritten rules and norms which guide how people are expected to behave. It is essential that the organisation's unspoken messages to employees match up with and back up its spoken messages. Unwritten beliefs and rules (even though often only based on tradition) are very difficult to change, but they have at least as much if not more effect on employee behaviour than do spoken and written rules.

Two aspects of culture to monitor for 'health' include:

1. People's receptiveness to 'problems':
   — Is bad news shared or is there a tendency to 'shoot the messenger'?
   — Is admitting to feeling stressed tantamount to admitting weakness, failure, or lack of capability?
   — Are staff and managers openly rewarded for bringing up problems and difficulties rather than for burying their heads?
2. The way that conflict is handled within the organisation:
   — Is conflict viewed as negative?
   — Is the environment overcompetitive? Is conflict seen as a situation in which one must win, or beat the other, rather than an opportunity for learning and growth? In such a climate, everyone is out for themselves, feeling a bit paranoid, always protecting themselves, being defensive and passing the buck.
   — Is conflict repressed, or smoothed over and avoided? Problems may be avoided temporarily, but under the surface are anger, discomfort and frustration.
   — Or are people always questioning in a non-blaming manner, looking for ways to improve? If managed properly, conflict can be a resource for better ideas and approaches.

Unstated messages about leadership are communicated through the ways in which managers are appraised and remunerated, in who is actually promoted, and who is spoken well of. It is important to consider how managers will be rewarded for making changes. Will managers really be rewarded or will they be subtly penalised for using counselling skills and for developing their employees? For example, is there a payoff for managers who empower and develop their subordinates to the point where they leave the department and move on to something else? Is the achievement acknowledged from above? Or does the manager's own department simply suffer from the loss? People are very much in tune with what they will be rewarded for in reality.

15

Counselling checklist

Now you have an understanding of how the counselling process works and what its benefits are, how using counselling skills can benefit you as a manager, and in which situations these skills can be applied.

Practising the components of counselling separately will build your confidence. You can practise pulling together the attitudes and skills in Parts II and III by informally counselling friends or relatives, as well as subordinates and colleagues. Use the following checklist to aid in preparation beforehand and to analyse your effectiveness afterward. Also ask those counselled for feedback on your skills. Do not forget to commend yourself on the items you performed well, as well as noting areas which need improvement – and be confident that your counselling skills *will* improve with practice!

Preparation

Have objectives for session firmly in mind (if meeting initiated ☐ by you).

Prepare paperwork (facts and information) if needed. ☐

Prepare physical surroundings: ☐
- Ensure privacy.
- Avoid interruptions.
- Arrange seating appropriately.
- Place clock strategically.

Opening

Extend warm greeting using the person's name. ☐

Set ground rules (time, confidentiality). ☐

'Hand over the floor' to the subordinate, verbally and non-verbally. ☐

If pre-disciplinary, clearly and concisely state reasons for meeting. ☐

Listening

Exhibit appropriate body language. ☐

Make eye contact. ☐

Use encouragers. ☐

Concentrate. ☐

Pay attention to subordinate's non-verbal communication. ☐

Reflect back thoughts and feelings to show empathy. ☐

Allow silences. ☐

Summarise. ☐

Questioning

Ask open questions. ☐

Ask closed questions when you need to direct the conversation, or to check facts. ☐

Ask probing questions to encourage expansion, elicit emotions. ☐

Do not ask too many probing questions one after the other. ☐

Ask questions to clarify and reflect. ☐

Avoid leading questions. ☐

Attitude

Create a safe atmosphere by showing empathy. ☐

Encourage talk about emotions. ☐

Do not be too: ☐
- directive/talkative;
- critical/judgemental;
- patronising;
- placating/oversympathetic.

Focus

Encourage talk about the person being counselled rather than other people. ☐

Identify underlying core problem(s). ☐

Intervene when subordinate waffles. ☐

Challenging

Do not challenge too early. ☐

Challenge tentatively. ☐

Try challenging by pulling first, before pushing. ☐

Preface challenging statements with empathetic ones. ☐

Problem solving

Accompany the person through the problem-solving or decision-making process. ☐

Try to get suggestions from them first. ☐

Make your suggestions tentatively in the form of questions. ☐

Ask open questions to get reactions to suggestions (both yours and theirs). ☐

Help them to uncover and work through blocks to action. ☐

Timing/pace

Be patient. ☐

Give the person space and time – except when necessary, do not push subordinate to move too fast. ☐

Do not attempt to accomplish too much in one meeting. ☐

Conclusion

Warn the person ahead when running out of time. ☐

Decide together future action/next steps. ☐

Summarise. ☐

Finish with a useful comment or constructive statement. ☐

Follow-up

PART V

Appendices

APPENDIX A

Resources

Training/Consulting

The author, Hilary Walmsley, can be reached through:
Kogan Page Limited
120 Pentonville Road
London N1 9JN

General Information

Association for Counselling at Work
British Association for Counselling
1 Regent Place
Rugby
Warwickshire CV21 2PJ
0788 578328 (information line)
0788 550899 (office)

Directories for Referral (Suggestions/Sources)

Counselling and Psychotherapy Resources Directory
British Association for Counselling
Rugby, Warwickshire, UK

Social Services Yearbook
Longman Group UK Ltd
Essex, UK

SEARCH Directory
BASW Trading Ltd
Birmingham, UK
Social services, consultancy and training directory.

Sources of Help Directory
The Mental Health Foundation
London (071)580-0145

Help To Hand
Nurse Practitioner Services Ltd
Essex, UK
Very comprehensive list of resources (not only medical).

Useful Telephone Numbers for Referral

Action on Smoking & Health
071-637 9843

Age Concern
081-640 5431

Alcoholics Anonymous
0904 644026

Cancerlink
071-833 2451

Catholic Marriage Advisory Council
071-371 1341

Citizens Advice Bureaux
071-351 2114

Divorce Conciliation & Advisory Service
071-730 2422

Eating Disorders Association
0603 767062

Gamblers Anonymous
071-837 7324

Legal Services Agency
041-353 3353

London Association of Bereavement Services
071-700 8134

MIND
071-727 8975

Narcotics Anonymous
071-498 9005

National Council for One Parent Families
071-267 1361

Relate: National Marriage Guidance
0788 573241

APPENDIX B

Bibliography

Jeoffrey Ahern, 'Counselling's Added Value', *Counselling At Work*, British Association for Counselling, Autumn 1993

'A Lead Body for Advice, Guidance, and Counselling', *Networks*, Advice, Guidance, and Counselling Lead Body, No. 1, March 1993

Tricia Allison, 'Counselling and Coaching', chapter from *The Handbook of Performance Management*, Institute of Personnel Management, London, 1991

Gordon Anderson, 'From Performance Appraisal to Performance Management', *Training and Development*, Oct 1993

Julia Berryman, *Developmental Psychology and You*, The British Psychological Society & Routledge, London, 1991

Frank Blackler and Sylvia Shimmin, *Applying Psychology In Organisations*, Methuen, London/New York, 1984

Robert Blake and Anne Adams McCanse, *Leadership Dilemmas – Group Solutions*, Gulf Publishing Co, Houston, 1991

Giles Burrows, *Redundancy Counselling for Managers*, Institute of Personnel Management, London, 1985

Ashley Callaghan, 'Counselling After Trauma', *Insight*, No. 19, June 1993

CEPEC, *Counselling at Work: Introducing and Using the Skills*, Kogan Page, London, 1988

CEPEC, *Life and Career – A Self-Development Workbook*, 1992

David Charles-Edwards, 'Human Leadership and Counselling in Organisations', *Counselling At Work*, British Association for Counselling, Summer 1993

Ian Cunningham, 'Someone to Watch Over Me', *Human Resources*, Winter 1992/3

Robert de Board, *Counselling People at Work*, Gower, Aldershot, 1983

Gerard Egan, *Exercises in Helping Skills*, Brooks/Cole, California, 1990

Hetty Einzig and Richard Evans (1990), *Personal Problems at Work, Counselling as a Resource for the Manager*, British Association for Counselling, London

Keith Elliot, 'Managerial Competencies', *Management Development*, Nov 1993

Daniel Feldman, *Managing Careers in Organisations*, Scott, Foresman and Co, Boston/London, 1988

Clive Fletcher, *Appraisal – Routes to Improved Performance*, Institute of Personnel Management, London, 1993

Elizabeth Foggo-Pays, *An Introductory Guide to Counselling*, Ravenswood Publications, Beckenham, 1983

Alan Fowler, 'How to Manage Cultural Change', *Personnel Management Plus*, Nov 1993

David Geldard, *Basic Personal Counselling* (2nd edn) Prentice Hall, Australia, 1993

Neil Glass, *Pro-Active Management*, Cassell Educational, London, 1991

Hiam, A (1993), *Does Quality Work? A Review of Relevant Studies*, The Conference Board, New York

Roger Holdsworth, 'Appraisal', chapter from *The Handbook of Performance Management*, Institute of Personnel Management, London, 1991

Barry Hopson and John Adams, *Transition; Understanding and Managing Personal Change*, Martin Robertson, 1976

Keith Hughes, *Retirement Counselling*, McGraw-Hill, Wokingham, 1993

David Johnson, 'Counselling Business Start-ups and Owner-managers of Small Firms', *Employee Counselling Today*, Vol 4 Issue 1, 1992

David Kolb, Irwin Rubin and James McIntyre, *Organisational Psychology*, Prentice Hall, NJ, 1984

Elisabeth Kubler-Ross, *Death: The Final Stage of Growth*, Prentice Hall, London, 1975

Frances Lee, 'Stress', *Personnel Today*, 7 Dec 1993

Stan Lester, 'Appraising the Performance Appraisal', *Training and Development*, Nov 1993

Edwin Lewis, *The Psychology of Counselling*, Holt, Rinehart and Winston, NY, 1970

John Lockett, *Effective Performance Management*, Kogan Page, London, 1992

Norman Maier, Allen Solem and Ayesha Maier, *The Role-Play Technique*, University Associates, La Jolla, CA, 1975

The Mental Health Foundation (1989), *Someone to Talk to at Work*, The Mental Health Foundation, London

The Mental Health Foundation (1993), *Mental Illness – The Fundamental Facts*, The Mental Health Foundation, London

Alan Mumford, *Management Development – Strategies for Action*, Institute of Personnel Management, London, 1993

E A Munroe, R J Manthei and J J Small (1983), *Counselling, A Skills Approach*, Methuen Publications Ltd, New Zealand

Frances Neale, *The Handbook of Performance Management*, Institute of Personnel Management, London, 1991

Richard Nelson-Jones, *Practical Counselling and Helping Skills*, Cassell Education, London, 1992

Robert Nicodemus, 'Facilitating Teamwork', *Counselling At Work*, British Association for Counselling, Winter 1993

Allan Pease, *Body Language*, Sheldon Press, London, 1981

Mike Pedler, John Burgoyne and Tom Boydell, *A Manager's Guide to Self-Development*, McGraw-Hill, London, 1986

Graham Pitts, 'Employee Assistance Programs', *Insight*, No. 19, June 1993

Sandy Pokras, *Systematic Problem-Solving and Decision-Making*, Kogan Page, London, 1989

L Rae, *The Skills of Interviewing*, Gower, Aldershot, UK, 1988

Michael Reddy, *The Manager's Guide to Counselling at Work*, The British Psychological Society and Methuen, Leicester/New York, 1987

Philip Sadler and Keith Milner, *The Talent-Intensive Organisation*, Economist Intelligence Unit, London, 1993

Lily Segerman-Peck, *Networking and Mentoring*, Piatkus, London, 1991

Mike Smith and Tony Vickers, 'And What About the Survivors?', *Training and Development*, Jan 1994

Paul Smith, 'An Intervention Assessment Model for Managers', *Counselling At Work*, British Association for Counselling, Winter 1993

Tim Steele, 'Preparing for the Worst', *Human Resources*, Summer 1993

R Tannenbaum and W H Schmidt, 'How to Choose a Leadership Style', *Harvard Business Review Monograph*, March–April 1958

Michael Thomas, 'What You Need to Know About Business Process Re-Engineering', *Personnel Management*, Jan 1994

Paul Thorne, *The New General Manager*, McGraw-Hill, Wokingham, 1989

Stuart Timperley and Keith Sisson, 'From Manpower Planning to Human Resource Planning', chapter from *Personnel Management in Britain*, edited by Keith Sisson, Basil Blackwell, 1989

Derek Torrington and Laura Hall, *Personnel Management*, Prentice Hall, Herts, 1991

Norman Toulson, *Preparing Staff for Retirement*, Gower, Aldershot, 1987

Peter Wallum, 'Succession Management', chapter from *The Handbook of Performance Management*, Institute of Personnel Management, London, 1991

Bridget Wright, 'Surviving Downsizing', *Counselling At Work*, British Association for Counselling, Winter 1993

Index